New Writing in Israel

Edited by Ezra Spicehandler
Co-edited by Curtis Arnson

SCHOCKEN BOOKS · NEW YORK

First published by SCHOCKEN BOOKS 1976

Library of Congress Cataloging in Publication Data
Main entry under title:

New Writing in Israel

1. Israeli literature — Translations into English.
2. English literature — Translation from Hebrew.
I. Spicehandler, Ezra.
PJ5059.EIN4   892.4'08'006   75-36497

Manufactured in Israel

New Writing in Israel

CONTENTS

FICTION

POETRY

Wartime in Leipzig

SHMUEL YOSEF AGNON

1

Since the day I came to live in Leipzig it was my habit to drop in on him often. And it was as though he was expecting me each time I entered his shop. If he was sitting and writing, he'd push pen and paper aside just to talk with me, if he was on the telephone, he'd cut short the conversation and pull up a chair for me to chat. And yet there was nothing about me, neither socially nor financially, to justify his attentions. In a city like Leipzig, where even rich ex-Lithuanian Talmud students looked askance at poor learned Jews, of what importance was a poor Jew like myself who wasn't even learned? It was remarkable, therefore, that Herr Lublin took such an interest in me. And it was remarkable too that while generally, when you visit someone often, you get to know him well, I knew no more about Herr Lublin, though I saw him all the time, than what he chose to tell me, so that any portrait I might sketch of him would simply consist of his own words. If he had been a leader in the

Jewish community, or if the free kitchen he'd donated to the army had been named after him, or the officers' club sponsored by his wife after her, I'd have no doubt heard gossip about them; but since deeds meant more to him than honor, he and his wife kept away from the public eye. Whatever I knew about him, then, I knew from him alone. And yet when I put everything that he had told me about himself together, I still couldn't make him out. Which is why the long talk I had with him that helped me to understand him better, one night when I came to congratulate him for having heard from his son who was in a prisoner-of-war camp, seemed like a gift from the blue.

Why a gift from the blue? Because if it hadn't been for the regular walks that I took every evening, and for my having run into the daughter of Herr Lublin's clerk Lemke on one of them, who told me that Herr Lublin had gotten a letter from his son in the prisoner camp, I'd have never gone to see him that night or heard what he had to say. I can remember it just as it happened, though I make no claim to quote him verbatim, as in passing from him to me, and from language to language, his words can't help but have changed.

But I'd better begin with my walks, and go from them to both the pertinent and impertinent facts about my encounter with Lemke's daughter, who told me of the letter that Herr Lublin received from his son, and leave for last my conversation with Herr Lublin himself, which took place at his office, and at the theater, and at the restaurant where we dined, and on our way back to his house and my room.

I had gone out for a walk in the streets of Leipzig, as I did every evening at twilight. I liked Leipzig and its crowds at that hour when the day ebbed away into night, much better than I did at midday, when the city often got on my nerves. With nightfall Leipzig put off the working day and the sky put on its stars. They weren't the same stars I remembered from the town where I was raised, or from the skies of Palestine, but a star was still a star, and I was grateful whenever one smiled on me far from home. They were really so small, and so outshone by the gas and electric lights of the city, that I might have been the only one to notice them at all. And as I like to acknowledge a favor, let me say this: if the shy stars above unassumingly kept their light to themselves, it's because they felt out of place in a place where men preferred earthlight and never even bothered looking up. If I hadn't been so unworthy of them, in fact, I'd have said they were shining just for me. And since such flights of fancy made me blush, I too was forced to look down.

Leipzig put off the working day and prepared for the working night. The days were too short; the war must go on, and the war needed new weapons every day. And so the days were made to run on into the nights. The day shift went off and the night shift went on. On feet that ached, in tattered clothes, in shoes that were cobbled and patched, the munitions workers passed each other in the street, their bodies one great pain. The wartime bread, though it filled no stomach, made everyone sick to the gills. The whole city was green from it and from everything else that it ate. And it was worse to be a munitions worker than a soldier who had fought in the war, because today's munitions workers would be tomorrow's soldiers, while yesterday's soldiers had already paid their dues, a hand or a foot perhaps, or some inconspicuous inner organ, and wore their medals on their chests like a note from the war that it was done with them. They bounced about on crutches and rubber legs, minus an arm or some other limb, their medals bouncing with them, and the young girls who saw the medals added their own fond glance. Not everyone came home from the war a hero, of course. While the heroes and their followers toured the city, other girls sat mourning other men. The war played favorites with its warriors. Some it let off with a limb or two, from others it took a whole life.

The streetlights were already lit. They came on all at once, before the daylight was done waning, as though by a single flash of luminance. The trolleys were lit too, as were the houses, the offices, and the shops. The display windows were lit with a special light of their own, because they were lined with mirrors that reflected the light from the street onto their goods. The trouble with these goods, though, was that they were no more real than reflections themselves. Let's leave unrealities, then, and light to those who make it, and talk about the latter instead. Somewhere in Leipzig sat a hidden man who switched on the gas and electric lights. The war had found him unworthy to serve it in battle and had made him a lighter of lights. It was he who lit the city and its people, and whose light fell on me as I walked. The strange thing was, though, that the more I walked his grandly lit streets of gas and electric, the more I thought of the little lights of the town where I was raised, of its candles, lanterns, and lamps.

The lanterns in our town were tin-and-glass boxes in each of which hung an oil lamp. There were lanterns on Mickiewicz Street, and on The Third of May Street, and in the new marketplace, and on Adam Asnyk Street, who was a poet born in our town, and by the house of my grandfather, may he rest in peace, and in several other places that have since been renamed. There was an old lantern by the main synagogue too, which hadn't been lit for ages, and about which all kinds of stories were told. No one in our town really needed the lanterns, because everyone knew the streets well, but the lanterns were lit all the same.

They were lit at the drop of night by a lame Pole with a ladder on his shoulders, who limped from lantern to lantern and lit each in its turn. Because he was lame, it was hard for him to stand on the ladder long enough to make sure that the oil wick had taken, so that the flame would sometimes go out by the time he'd climbed down. He'd never climb back up to relight it, though, because so many other lanterns were still waiting to be lit. There was a saying in our town that the only reason that the lamps were ever lit was for people to see that they weren't. Watching the lame Pole climb the ladder made me wonder why he had been given such a job: didn't our town fathers have the heart not to make a lame man climb a ladder he couldn't stand on? Now that a war was loose in the world and had scattered our town to the wind, there probably wasn't a single lantern left there. Even if there was, it probably wasn't working, and even if it worked, there was probably no one and no oil to light it. But why talk just about the lanterns? The lights were out in the houses, and courtyards, and synagogues, and study halls too; as there wasn't a Jew left in town, there wasn't a spark of light either. And yet Leipzig was flooded with light. It may not have had stars like our town did, but it had gas and electric enough.

There was a habit in our town of calling all fine merchandise "Lapsig" goods, which is how our townsmen said Leipzig. And now here I was, a townsman from our town, looking at such goods in the windows. Because of the war, though, there weren't any good goods left. The war had taken them all, and what it had missed the profiteers hadn't so that ersatz of ersatz was all you could get. And yet Leipzig was still Leipzig, and even its ersatz was still something.

I stopped by a display window to look at some pens, the kind that people called fountain pens but that I call miracle pens. And it really was a miracle that a pen should be its own inkstand, so that one didn't have to waste precious time dipping it in ink. With a little inspiration from above, I thought, one might even write something good with it. I thought that about myself, because I sometimes dabbled in writing.

Next to the pens were all kinds of paper, and next to the paper were different sizes of notebooks and writing pads, large, small, long, wide, thin, and fat. My own desk had once been piled with such things when I had worked on my dissertation on clothes, but now that I'd put my dissertation aside, my desk had plenty of room. Concerning my dissertation, I couldn't say that I missed it and I couldn't say that I didn't. The fact of the matter was that since I'd put it aside, I was much freer to do what I wanted.

And what was it that I wanted?

I knew at least partly what it was; and this was in part to resume my Jewish studies, which I'd deserted in order to live in Berlin and work on my dissertation, and which had deserted me too. Now I had put both Berlin and my dissertation behind me and had come to Leipzig hoping that I and Rabbi Yonatan might scamper through the Talmud together — but Rabbi Yonatan was busy with his teaching and his rabbinical courts and had no time to scamper. And so I was a man of leisure who could leave things to whim or blind chance. I walked the streets of Leipzig like a castaway of the times, stopping by every show window to see what it contained. The windows were show windows, all right, but they had little to show for themselves. The war had taken it all, and what it hadn't, the profiteers had. Ersatz of ersatz was all that was left. Even the shoppers were ersatz, because whoever wasn't had been taken off to war.

Oh, yes: there were also three or four days a week that I spent in the Orientalia and Semitica Bookstore of old Thomas Caspar Marius & Sons. It was a huge store, with more books than met the eye, many of which were new to me and some of which were not. If you ask me how I got to Thomas Caspar Marius & Sons' bookstore, I'd have to tell you it was through Professor Nadelstecher, since it was at Nadelstecher's house that I met old Herr Marius. But I'd also have to tell you that old Marius took me on only because he didn't ask Nadelstecher to recommend me, which Nadelstecher wouldn't have done, because he'd have feared that if I worked for Herr Marius, I'd have told him that many of Nadelstecher's scholarly discoveries were actually mine. And yet the fact of the matter was that Nadelstecher had no need to worry, because he knew perfectly well that in all the time I'd spent with him I'd never so much as breathed a word about his stealing my ideas. In any case, I was introduced to Herr Marius, who invited me to visit his store, which I did. He received me graciously and we had a pleasant chat, at the end of which he asked a clerk to bring him some books he had recently acquired, some of which I'd never even heard of. As I was leaving, he asked me if I might want to look at them once more. "*Once* more?" I said. "A hundred times wouldn't be enough." "In that case," he said, "come as often as you like." By the time we finally parted, he'd offered me a salary to be in charge of his Hebraica collection. After I'd worked there a while he asked if I'd put in an additional day, to which I agreed, which meant that I now worked there four days a week, rummaging through volumes that had lain about since the days of old Thomas Caspar Marius' great-great-grandfather, who bequeathed his name to the store and to the Thomas Caspar Marius' whom I knew.

And so I worked in the Judaica and Hebraica room of
Thomas Caspar Marius' Orientalia and Semitica Bookstore,
sitting at a long table surrounded by books which I indexed
by subject and name. The contents of some of them were
evident at a glance, while those of others evaded me more
the longer I looked at them, even when they had a title page
in good condition with the author's and publisher's names
on it and the date and place of publication. Some books I
couldn't make out because these names meant nothing to
me, some because I knew that in the year and place of
publication there was such a massacre of Jews that no one
could have put out a Hebrew book. Not that I was any great
bibliograph when it came to Hebraica, but I had seen my
share of Hebrew books and had a good head for names.
Whenever I came across such a book, I wouldn't put it down
until I at least had some notion of who had written it and
when. And it was to old Herr Marius' credit that it never
bothered him to see me sitting day after day over the very
same book. On the contrary, I could tell that it pleased him
that I wasn't dismissing his books with a glance.

2

What was true of old Herr Marius, however, wasn't true of
all his staff. Once it happened that I spent three whole days
going over a book that I couldn't decipher. I resolved to
return to it the next day. I did, and I still couldn't make it
out, so I resolved to return to it again. That night Gerti
Hennings came to my room. I must have looked surprised
by her visit. "When a person is alone in his room at night,"
explained Gerti Hennings, "he sometimes thinks of things

that he doesn't when he's with people during the day." It was the only time she ever came to my room, and she did so only because of Herr Marius' bookstore where she worked. Why do I bother to mention it? Because of Lise Lotte Lemke, who once cattily asked me if it was true that that croaking little frog of a songwriter was a frequent guest in my room.

I never heard Lise Lotte Lemke, who was the daughter of Lemke's wife, croak any songs herself, but you were even more likely to read about her in the newspapers than you were to find one of Gerti Hennings' songs there. And she certainly wasn't fishing for an invitation from me, because she had all the rich young suitors she could want. The one thing she had in common with Gerti Hennings was that whenever she saw me, she'd open her purse and pull out some newspaper with her name in it to show me. And if I didn't have the patience to read what was written there, she'd read it to me herself. If I know anything about athletics, indeed, it's only because of those articles, as Lise Lotte Lemke was a champion athlete who was always being written up in the sports pages. There was no tearing myself away from her until I'd read or heard every word.

It wasn't through Lemke that I came to know Lise Lotte Lemke, it was through Kalman Leibusch Hoenig. Lise Lotte Lemke and Kalman Leibusch Hoenig's daughter, Regina Hoenig were friends. Once when Lise Lotte went to visit Regina she found Kalman Leibusch at home by himself. As he was a pious Jew, to whom it's forbidden to be alone with an unmarried woman, he went and stood by the window. I happened to be passing by in the street and he signaled me to come up. "You know," he said when I did, "I was reading something in a commentary last Sabbath that I've been wanting to show you." He went to another room to

fetch the book, and while I was waiting for him, I began to
talk with Lise Lotte. She must have heard from her mother
that I was a friend of Herr Lublin's and taken me for a
wealthy bachelor, because she was accustomed to the
company of rich young Jews.

Lise Lotte wasn't like her mother or her mother's
husband, who had learned to make do with what they had;
what she had, it was true, she didn't lose hold of, but her
grasp was even greater than her grip, and extended not just
to sports, but to the patrons of sports as well. The most
eligible young men of Leipzig, the sons of the city's great
merchants, its downtown princes and courtiers, were all at
her beck and call, like slaves before their master, or, to
change the gender of the simile, like bondmaidens before
their mistress. It used to be said of Lise Lotte that one of
them meant no more to her than another, that is, that she
had no favorites among them, until one was killed in the
war and all knew she had cared for him most.

I never knew the young man, of whom I first heard when
he was killed, a common occurrence in those days when the
nation's best youth was being slain. Just two or three days
previously, however, I had made his father's acquaintance.
It so happened that I had stepped into the Brody Synagogue
one Sabbath for the afternoon prayer, and as I chanced to
be the only Levite there, I was called to recite the Levite's
blessing over the Torah. After the service, the sexton
whispered to me that I should thank the presiding chairman
of the synagogue for having granted me the honor. The
presiding chairman that month happened to be the boy's
father. Some time later, when I stopped by his place of
business, he remembered me from that Sabbath and struck
up a conversation.

What brought me to his place of business? The Sabbath

beforehand he had gone to a girl's confirmation party and had run into Herr Lublin's wife Nora, whom he lauded for having sponsored her officers' club, which was a credit to the Jewish people, since it was yet another proof of Jewish dedication to Germany's war effort, which was already so great in money and in lives and even in both together, as was the case with the Lublins themselves, who had sent their two sons off to war and their daughter to work in a hospital for war casualties, besides having given so freely of their fortune to Germany's brave soldiers, Herr Lublin with his army kitchen, and Frau Lublin with her officers' club. It actually made him envious, on account of which he wished to contribute a modest sum himself, whose exact amount, however, he wouldn't state on the Sabbath so as not to violate the spirituality of the day. Should Frau Lublin be downtown some day, perhaps she might stop by his business, and he would see to the matter at once. A few days later she went to collect his pledge and invited me along. He rubbed his hands with pleasure when he saw me and launched into a speech about the war and every man's duty to the Fatherland, especially every Jew's. He himself, it so happened, was not a German but an Austrian, and not really an Austrian either but a Jew from Galicia, but since Germany had been good to him and had made him a citizen, he felt every bit as German as the next man. Above all, it was as a Jew loyal to his God and his faith that he felt obliged to do the utmost for Germany. He had given a son to the war, and was only too glad to give money even before being asked. ... After writing Frau Lublin her check, he began to talk in praise of his son, who had taken his prayer book and phylacteries to the battlefield with him; God, he was sure, would reward such a display of devotion by bringing the boy home safe and sound and finding a good

Jewish girl for him to settle down with. Of course he had no way of knowing that his son was already dead.

I've gotten on to the subject of the father because of the son, and on to the son because of Lise Lotte Lemke, on account of whom I first heard of him. Lise Lotte Lemke I first met in Kalman Leibusch Hoenig's house, who invited me up because he didn't wish to be alone with her, even though she was a friend of his daughter's. Because of all these becauses, then, I'd better say something about Regina Hoenig. Regina resembled neither Lise Lotte Lemke nor Gerti Hennings. Lise Lotte worked in a travel agency but thought only about sports, which was all she lived and breathed for. Each of the young men who showered her with clothing, hats, perfume, and jewelry was sure that she cared for him, but Lise Lotte cared only for the sports pages and what it said about her there. It was no exaggeration to say that two lines in a newspaper meant more to her than ten suitors with their clothes and eau de Cologne. The most foolish thing her mother Friederike ever did was let a young actor in the itinerant theater troupe she was in get her pregnant, because the director threw them both out of the company, and the young man had to go to work as a clerk in Herr Lublin's business. Lise Lotte wasn't going to do any man favors who didn't first offer to wed her legally by Christian or Jewish law. Once, three or four generations ago, Christian families had been happy to marry their daughters to Jews, who made good husbands and didn't beat their wives or get drunk. Anti-Semitism had changed all that, but there were still plenty of girls on the lookout for Jewish husbands, provided, of course, they were rich.

As for Gerti Hennings, whom Lise Lotte Lemke called a croaking frog of a songwriter, she worked in the bibliographical department of old Herr Thomas Caspar Marius &

Sons' Semitica and Orientalia Bookstore. Her mother was
Goetz Weigel's granddaughter, while her father was an
official in the Anti-Bribery Society. Prior to the war Herr
Hennings had led a life of leisure: he had spent much time
at home with his wife and daughter, had dropped in at the
pub twice a week to drink beer with his friends, and on
Sundays, needless to say, had gone out walking and
shooting. Since the outbreak of the war, however, he'd been
swamped by the demands of his job. There was no end to
rumored and reported bribes, one day's suspicion became
the next day's hard fact, yet there was no way you could
manage to convict anyone of anything, because the
witnesses were all away at war, or worse yet, had already
been killed there. In either case, the letters kept piling up on
his desk faster than he could file them, so that by the time
he got home to his family at night, he was too weary even
to speak. If there was any consolation regarding Gerti, it
was the realization that he had falsely suspected his wife of
conceiving her by another man. With each passing day her
resemblance to him grew clearer, both in her shortness and
her nearsightedness, which were the two reasons that the
war had left him alone and not taken him off to the front.
The one thing he couldn't get over was the lyrics that she
wrote. Where had she gotten the talent for them from?
Certainly not from him or her mother. Yet whenever he was
sitting in the pub with his friends, and they lifted their
voices together in some song which he knew that Gerti had
written, his doubts would leave him at once, and he would
join in the chorus, proud of his daughter who had such a
gift.

    Regina Hoenig, as I've said, was like neither Gerti
Hennings nor Lise Lotte Lemke. Lise Lotte worked in a
travel agency but cared only for sports; Gerti Hennings

wrote patriotic lyrics yet worked in the bibliographical department of old Herr Marius' bookstore; Regina Hoenig kept busy at home. She helped her mother with the cooking and the housework, her six sisters with their homework from school, and her father with his business correspondence and his books. Whatever she did, she did well, so that she was well-liked by everyone, by the more discriminating because of her brains, and by the less because of her friendly dark eyes, which really weren't so dark but were only made to seem so by the black curl that tumbled down over them. This misconception reached such an absurd point that an admiring poet even wrote some verses for her wedding night praising her dark eyes, which he compared to dewy light (the same poet was also mistaken when he compared her stature to a palm tree's, since she was really only average height). Regina helped her father not only in his business but in his spiritual pleasures as well, for each Saturday night, when his Hasidic friends gathered for a meal at his house and sang farewell hymns to the departing Sabbath queen, she took out her violin and accompanied them. Who taught her to play the violin? She had learned herself, just as she had learned other skills. Hasidic families from Leipzig, Chemnitz, Plauen and Dresden all sought her hand for their sons — and yet she had already been promised to someone. To whom, you ask, and how come? To the son of a favorite disciple of the rabbi to whom her father and his friends owed allegiance, who had chosen her himself for the match.

What happened was, back in the days when peace still reigned in the world, his rabbi had gone every summer to a certain health spa in Germany. Once he stopped off in Leipzig on his way, where he stayed with Kalman Leibusch Hoenig. Every morning Regina, who was only nine years old then and wasn't called Regina but Rikel, brought him his cup of coffee and his bowl of little cakes. So nicely did she say "amen" each time he blessed them before eating that he took a fancy to her and chose her for a favorite disciple's son. And as soon as he came of age, Kalman Leibusch married her off.

I was at the wedding. So were all of Kalman Leibusch's friends, and other Hasidim of other rival rabbis who had made peace among themselves in honor of the occasion. The wedding jester recited the tale of Reb Yudel Hasid in elegant song and verse, while his three daughters and the musicians accompanied him on their instruments. The applause hadn't died down when one of the wedding guests rose to his feet and began to improvise some rhymes about the faithful young couple, who had waited impatiently for the happy day when God would make them man-and-wife. As soon as his poem was over, the elders of the Hasidim performed the customary wedding dance with the bride. Their wives kicked up their heels too, and so engrossed were all in the happy event, the joyous celebration of which was a great commandment, that they forgot about their own sons, whose lives hung in the balance of war. Next came the turn of the other important guests to dance with the bride, and then of the ordinary guests, of whom I too was one. I held one end of the handkerchief, she held the other, and we danced as we were commanded to, I averting my eyes from her so as not to look at another man's wife, she averting her eyes from me so as not to look at another man, while the jester called out his jests to the accompaniment of the musicians. A fine time was had at Regina's wedding, and everyone enjoyed himself so much that the war was all but forgotten. Within two weeks she left her husband and ran off with one of the musicians who had played at her

wedding. The same rabbi who married her divorced her, and
ninety-nine days later married her again.

There was yet another young lady I should mention. I
met her at the home of Rabbi Yonatan, who told me her
story. Her name was Ilschen Tommer, and there was
nothing special about her, except that she was a Christian
and had problems, because the young man she wished to
marry was a Jew of the priestly caste, and a priest is
forbidden to marry a non-Jew even if she becomes Jewish.
Ilschen had been drawn to Jewish things even as a small
child. There wasn't a Jewish holiday on which she hadn't
stood outside the synagogue to listen to the prayers, and
having reached adulthood, her one desire was to become
Jewish herself. In the end she heard that in Leipzig there
was a Jewish boy who hadn't been drafted because he was
an invalid and slightly touched in the head. Well then,
thought Ilschen, I'll marry him, and that's how I'll become a
Jew. But no one would agree to convert her, the Orthodox
rabbis because of her motives, the Reform rabbis because
they feared the wrath of the Orthodox. The boy's mother
made the rounds of all four Jewish congregations in Leipzig,
Reform, Orthodox, Ultraorthodox, and Galician-Hasidic
whose synagogue was named after Hindenburg, begging
mercy for her son, who needed a wife and couldn't find
one, since no self-respecting Jewish girl would marry an
invalid. The rabbis all rejected her, each for reasons of his
own, while she shouted at each that he had no compassion,
not even for widows and orphans.

3

I felt I'd had enough of wandering the city, and of my
wandering thoughts and decided to visit Rabbi Yonatan, on

whose account I had settled in Leipzig. Not that the number of pages of Talmud I had managed to study in Leipzig would warm a pious student's heart, but I still hadn't abandoned my hopes.

Had I cut through the narrow back streets that were a short-cut to his home, I would have gotten there quickly enough. But because my thoughts continued to wander, I let my feet take me along busy avenues all the way to the railway station, where I found myself trapped in a great throng of men and women. When I finally fought free of it, I was standing next to Lise Lotte Lemke, who had just gotten off a train.

"Have you been out of town?" I asked her.

"That's just what I was about to ask you," she said.

"How is that?"

"Because," said Lise Lotte Lemke, "no one ever sees you any more. I've been wanting to visit you, but I didn't know how, because no one even knows where you live. Regina Hoenig says that you take your room with you in your pocket when you leave it."

"That," I said, "is an exaggeration. As small as my room is, my pocket is even smaller. How is your leg feeling?"

"I've forgotten I ever sprained it," said Lise Lotte. "But I'll never forget that if you hadn't picked me up off the sidewalk and supported me all the way home on your arm, I'd be lying there to this day." She linked arms with me and said: "Come on home with me, and I'll show you some-thing. Aren't you curious to know what it is?"

"I wasn't sure it was proper to ask yet," I said. "Well, what is it?"

"It's a photograph of me the day I beat the Halle team. You were there to see me win that time, weren't you? Come home with me and I'll show it to you in the paper."

"I'd be glad to," I said, "except that. . . ."

"Yes, I know," she interrupted. "Except that that little worm who works with you among old Marius' books is waiting for you."

"Except that Herr Lublin is waiting for me," I said.

"If Herr Lublin is waiting for you," she said, letting go of my arm, "who am I to detain you? I suppose you must be going to congratulate him."

"Why, has his daughter gotten engaged?" I asked.

"It wouldn't surprise me if she has," said Lise Lotte. "And if she hasn't, she will soon enough. Rich girls have a way of getting engaged. When father produces the dowry, the young men produce themselves."

"I can see, Fraulein Lemke," I said, "that I'm not going to get anything out of you. I'd better go ask Herr Lublin himself."

"Well, well," said Lise Lotte. "So there's something that Herr Lublin's clerk's daughter knows that Herr Lublin's friend doesn't!"

I shook her hand to say goodbye.

"Wait," she said, holding on to me. "I'll come with you. We're going the same way. You've forgotten that I live in Herr Lublin's courtyard."

I retraced the streets that had brought me to Lise Lotte Lemke, until together we reached the vicinity of Herr Lublin's store. Most of the shops along the way were shut already, especially in Goldmakers Lane next to Boettiger Street, where they always closed early. The little lane was a silent, breathless presence, lit only by the muffled glow of an old street lamp.

I wanted to say something, the way one sometimes does when one finds himself in a quiet place, but I didn't, because the quiet infected me too.

"But I want you to look at me!" said Lise Lotte.

I looked at her without knowing what she meant.

"You're still not really looking," she said.

I looked and still I didn't know. Suddenly she bent over and seemed to spread out. She huffed and puffed and pitched about like a woman immersed in rolls of fat. If I hadn't known her, I'd have taken her for a middle-aged lady of forty or more.

"You're still seeing Lise Lotte," said Lise Lotte, "but in a minute I'm going to show you Mother Friederike. This morning Mother Friederike read in the newspaper about a shipment of frozen meat that arrived from Poland or Russia or some other place that we Germans have conquered. She put on her long coat and ran to the marketplace as fast as she could, in order to get there before the other women of Leipzig, all of whom are dying for a fatty piece of meat. As soon as she got to the marketplace, she began to sniff about the stalls. Suddenly she smelled a pipe tobacco that she remembered from the days when she was still a prima donna. She looked around and saw a man tapping his pipe against a counter to empty out the ashes. He felt her staring at him and said, "Woman, your nose is sticking to my mustache!' 'Ay, ay, ay,' said Mother Friederike, 'who is it I see if not Herr Direktor Ehmichen?' 'And who is it I see?' asked Herr Direktor Ehmichen. 'Can it be,' said Mother Friederike, 'that you've forgotten Friederike Drangsal?' 'You're not one Friederike,' said Herr Direktor Ehmichen, 'you're enough for two-and-a-half.' 'Please don't make fun of me, Herr Direktor,' said Mother Friederike. 'May I hope to die if I'm making fun of you,' said Herr Direktor Ehmichen, 'but it's beyond me how a slim thing like you could have doubled and redoubled itself.' 'I'd be honored if you'd come have a cup of coffee with us at home, Herr Direktor,' said Mother Friederike. 'Perhaps you'd like me to give your Lemke another taste of my boot in his rear?' asked Herr Direktor Ehmichen. 'Ah, Herr Direktor,' said Mother Friederike, giving him one of her looks, 'I can see that you haven't forgotten your Friederike after all.' "

Lise Lotte gave me one of her looks and said, "I can see that you don't even know who Herr Direktor Ehmichen is. Ehmichen is the man in whose company Mother Friederike was the prima donna and Father Lemke was an actor too. And if Father Lemke hadn't butted in between Mother and Herr Direktor Ehmichen, I'd be an Ehmichen today and not a Lemke. But since I'm only a Lemke, and Lemke is Herr Lublin's clerk, and Herr Lublin is waiting for you, far be it from me to tell you to forget about Herr Lublin and come see my photograph. Because you know, this wartime paper that they print on is so rotten that by tomorrow it will just be yellow dust."

I asked Lise Lotte Lemke again why she had supposed that I was going to congratulate Herr Lublin.

"Herr Lublin," said Lise Lotte, "just got a letter through the Red Cross from his son in the prisoner-of-war camp."

I bade Lise Lotte goodbye and went to see Herr Lublin.

4

I cut down Goldmakers Lane, making a detour around the four shops in order to avoid the belt maker, who never let me go once he managed to get hold of me. He was a harassed and troubled soul, the belt maker, and at a loss what to do with himself, for he was all but overwhelmed by a sense of sin, and was convinced that somewhere in the world there must be a true faith, since God couldn't possibly have left all His creatures without one, and that He must have revealed it to someone, perhaps to those same Hebrews he had seen in the Saracen lands where he had wandered long ago with a friend as a young journeyman. And since I was a Hebrew too, he was always happy to speak with me, in the hope that I might make him see the light. In actual fact, it was he who did all the talking, while I simply listened in silence, but the wild sparks thrown off by his own imagination persuaded him that I must be arguing too. "If I follow what you say," he would say to me, or, "if I understand you correctly," whereas I had never said anything, and he only thought that I had. I made a point of saying nothing, indeed, because I never discussed religion with Gentiles, who were always looking for converts and putting words in Jews' mouths. "Look," I once said to him, "I know nothing about theology: what I learned from my forefathers, who learned from their forefathers, and so on and so forth back to Moses at Mount Sinai, is enough for me, and I can only hope to be as worthy as they were to keep the Law in perfect faith and desire." Yet if I thought this would discourage him from pressing me further, I was wrong.

"You needn't try telling me that," he said. "If I told you all I knew about you, you wouldn't try to pretend."

"I don't know what it is that you know about me," I answered, "or why you think I'm pretending, but let's hear what you have to say."

He didn't say anything.

"There was something you wanted to tell me," I prompted. "What was it?"

He looked at me once, and then again, and said nothing. Perhaps he already regretted having spoken, or perhaps he had forgotten, or perhaps he was thinking it over. Who on earth could tell with an old man like that? I cupped my left hand and began counting my fingers, determined to take my leave of him as soon as I reached ten. Before I did, however, I looked at him once more. He shut his eyes and said:

"One night in a dream I saw a garden full of trees. One of them was a fruit tree, and beneath it sat a man giving out fruit to all who were standing there. I reached out for some too. But before I was given any, I awoke."

"So?" I said.

"For years," he said, opening his eyes, "I tried to understand the dream. Who was the man I saw sitting beneath the tree, and why did he haunt me so? There were times when I despaired of understanding it, and times when I overcame my despair. There were times when I lost all hope of ever knowing who was the man giving out fruit beneath the tree, and times when I was sure I'd find out. One day I was sitting and working in my shop when I saw a young fellow talking to Weizelrode. I put down my work and sat there wondering, because Weizelrode didn't speak to anyone, let alone conduct a conversation. After a while the two of them entered his shop and didn't come out. And I hadn't seen anyone enter Weizelrode's shop in ages, because Weizelrode never let anyone set foot in it. An hour went by, and then another. I began to think I should call the police, because who knew what might be happening in there? We had a case over on Gottsched Street, you know: there was a Jew named Stern who sold jewelry there, and one day a carriage pulled by four horses stopped by his store, and out stepped a fine lady in fancy clothes with all kinds of ribbons and bows, and two maids-in-waiting to hold up the train of her dress, and they all went into Stern's store. A few hours later they found Stern unconscious and everything gone from his store. So I said to my neighbor the knife grinder, 'Peter,' I said, 'have you seen what I've seen?' 'No, I haven't,' he said, 'and I don't want to either. I've seen enough of him as it is, every day for sixty years, and if the English or the French or the Russians don't drop a bomb on him, I'll have to see him for sixty years more, because he'll never die of his own free will.' A few hours later the two of them came out of the store. This time I got a good look at the young fellow, and I recognized him as soon as I did: it was the same man who sat beneath the tree in the garden giving out fruit. The damnedest thing about it, though, was that beneath the tree in my dream he'd seemed old, while coming out of Weizelrode's shop he was a youngster."

"I still don't see the connection," I said, "between the man in the garden and my remarks about theology."

The belt maker laughed sadly. "So you still won't admit who you are. It's you who went into Weizelrode's shop, and it's you who sat beneath the tree in the garden giving out fruit."

"Beneath the tree in the garden," I said, repeating his words. I didn't repeat them mockingly, or questioningly, but encouragingly, as one sometimes does in the middle of a story to remind the storyteller where he is.

The belt maker took his long beard in his hand and looked at me open-eyed. Yet even while he looked his eyelids drooped again and his left hand, which held his beard, grew limp. His voice, however, was clear. It didn't sound tired at all, and it had a musical lilt like a preacher's.

"The garden is the world, and the trees of the garden are the different beliefs, and the fruit tree is a symbol of the true faith, and you sat beneath it in the garden giving out fruit to all who were standing there."

"I really don't remember it," I said. "When did it

happen? I mean, when did you dream it? You did say you dreamed it, didn't you?"

"I dreamed it. And what God showed me in my dream He has shown me awake. It took many bitter years to come to it, but now I've seen by day what I saw in my dream by night."

"When did you dream it?" I asked again.

"When did I dream it? In the Saracen lands, when I was wandering through the world with my friend as a young journeyman."

"That would make it at least seventy years ago." I said.

"Most likely it would," he said.

"And how old do you think I am?" I asked. "I'll tell you exactly: twenty-seven years and four months."

"I was sleeping that night in the attic of a Jewish fruit dealer," he went on, "who wasn't at all like the Jews here in Leipzig. Suddenly I saw a great garden several miles wide, like the distance from Leipzig to Koeniz and back again, and the garden had many, many trees, yet none had fruit but the one beneath which you sat, giving it out to all who were standing there. And when I reached out to take some, I awoke. I looked for you a long, long time before I found you at Weizelrode's, but I knew you the moment I saw you from that tree in the garden. You sat beneath it giving out fruit to all who were standing there, but I didn't get any when I reached for it."

I wondered what to say to the old man. In the end I said: "You're more fortunate than those who received the fruit in the dream, because they awoke to find nothing in their hands, while you had nothing to begin with and were spared their disappointment."

"I was spared disappointment," he nodded, "but not long years of hope."

"Who doesn't suffer from hope?" I asked.

"We suffer from many things," he laughed sadly.

"But of all sufferers," I said, "I know of none greater than the sufferer of faith."

"The sufferer who has faith but doesn't know in what!" he shouted in sudden wrath.

I thought of the verse, "Be quiet unto the Lord and submit to Him." Had he been a Jew, I might have said to him, "Wait for the salvation of the Lord."

"Goodbye," I said instead, and I took my leave of him.

Perhaps it was wrong of me to have left him like that, and perhaps it wasn't. Whatever favors and explanations Jews grant to Gentiles, they always turn out badly for the Jews. And in any case, I'd said goodbye to him in Hebrew, *shalom*, which meant peace, and there was no better blessing than that.

5

I walked in on Herr Lublin and found him sitting before a pile of letters. He looked up and said: "I'm glad that you've come. If you hadn't, I'd have had to go looking for you."

He pushed aside the letters and leafed through some papers on his desk. "Here," he said, holding up a sheaf of tickets. "I've been sent some tickets for the theater. They're for opening night. You want to know what the name of the play is? It wouldn't mean anything to you."

I looked at Herr Lublin in surprise. He had never talked to me about the theater before, and now he wanted me to come with him to a premier. But I checked myself and congratulated him first on the letter he'd received from his son, and asked that he relay my best wishes to Frau Lublin too. He didn't react. How many times, after all, could he say thank you to each congratulation? Mine certainly wasn't the first. Here you are, I thought to myself, sitting and saying nothing when a man has just heard from his son in an enemy prison camp! You might at least look up at him. But I didn't look up, because my thoughts kept running from father to son, and from son back to father again.

"Neither my wife nor my daughter can come to the theater with me," Herr Lublin said. "My wife can't come because she still isn't over the shock. The letter came suddenly, and now she feels worse than ever about her son being a prisoner, because it's taken on a reality that it never had for her before. And my daughter can't come because they're arranging some kind of musical evening tonight for the soldiers at the hospital where she works. So I'm the only Lublin still available to see the play. You'd be easing the burden for me if you'd come to see it with me."

"A ticket for opening night!" I said to Herr Lublin. "It's a gift from the blue. I haven't been to the theater since coming to Leipzig."

Herr Lublin picked up the telephone and reserved a table for two after the show at Glueckstock's restaurant, where the local gourmets liked to eat. "If the play is as short as most modern plays are," he said, putting down the receiver, "and that's the one good thing about them, we'll get to the restaurant in time. In general," he went on, "I'm not much of a theater-goer. If my wife insists on dragging me, I go. Tonight, though, I'm going because she can't go, that is, because she asked me to go in her place, since she's something of a patron of the playwright's and helped him to get the play produced. In fact, I suspect her of having had even more of a hand in it than that, and of having supplied him with part of the plot. For all I know, she even helped him write it. Before the war, you know, Nora used to write plays, and it was always a happy occasion for the family when she read one of them out loud. Sometimes she'd even give me a private reading. I wasn't much of a judge of them, though. I'm a busy man, and even when I tried to listen, I couldn't really concentrate. You can't find me the woman, no matter how smart, who knows how to pick an hour when her husband has time to listen to everything she has to say."

Herr Lublin passed a hand over his brow and continued:

"Sometimes when I'm in the theater with my wife, and we're watching some play of the sort she's particularly fond of, I say to myself thank God that she hasn't published any of her own. There's nothing wrong with a woman writing poetry, or playing the piano, or even the violin, but to start telling the whole world about what goes on in her bedroom. . . ."

The ring of the telephone interrupted him. "Yes, darling," he said into it, "I haven't forgotten. You can rest assured. I promised you, and I will."

"I promised my wife to go to the theater tonight," said Herr Lublin to me, hanging up, "and she was calling to remind me. To tell you the truth, I don't think it's because of the letter from our son that she isn't going tonight, I think it's because she's afraid her close friends will notice that the play is about the life of Nora Nachhut before she married me. If you ask my opinion, though, she's got nothing to worry about. I'm willing to bet on the author that he's put so much poetry into it that no one will recognize anything. And because his feelings mustn't be hurt, since Nora Nachhut was so kind as to be his patron, I have to go see the damned thing. Well, let's have a drink, and be off."

Herr Lublin produced a bottle of cognac and filled two glasses that were standing on the table, one for him and one for me. "I like a good glass of wine," he said, " and a good mug of beer too, but when it comes to cognac, I have to grit my teeth. *L'hayyim!* Another glass? No? Well then, let's go. There's really no need to rush, though. I have to drink this cognac on doctor's orders, but it's really just laziness on his part. He gets so tired of writing prescriptions that he tells me to drink cognac instead. It's supposed to be good for my heart."

Herr Lublin's eyes twinkled. "I just thought of a nice story," he said, "which I'm sure you'll enjoy if you haven't heard it already, because it's about your grandfather. Someone recently told me that he had died, but the story is alive and well."

To the story that Herr Lublin told me I will add what I myself heard in my native town and combine the two versions:

Our family had a relative in Vienna, a professor in the university there, which was not a position reached by many Jews in those days. All of Galician Jewry was proud of him, to say nothing of my grandfather, who had helped him during his student days by supporting his widowed mother. How did it happen? After the future professor's father died, my grandfather took the widow into his house and paid for her upkeep and needs, thus relieving her three sons of the responsibility for her so that they could look after themselves. Two of them started a printing press and a bookstore, while the third continued his studies, which at first were still Jewish but later became secular. He continued to remember my grandfather's kindness and used to send him greeting cards from Vienna and a copy of every book that he published. Once he became a professor and earned a handsome living, he began sending gifts as well, especially on Purim. Each gift was something special, a nice piece of kitchenware or some unusual food. Once he sent an amber pipe, which my grandfather smoked on holidays; the exotic fruits over which we said the *shehechiyanu* blessing on the second day of Rosh Hashanah also came from him.

One Purim the professor sent my grandfather a gift package with a bottle of liquor in it. My grandfather suspected it might be wine produced by Gentiles, which is forbidden to Jews, so he put it away in the cellar. After the Passover he thought of it again. It occurred to him then that it might not be wine at all, but some sort of brandy, yet if it was brandy he could no longer drink it either, since being a fermented drink made it like leavened bread, which it was impermissible to consume if it dated from before the Passover and hadn't been sold to a Gentile and rebought from him. On the other hand, he couldn't spill it out either, since in case it was kosher he would be wasting good food, which was also a sin. Neither could he simply leave it in the cellar, since it if was brandy it had to be disposed of at once.

"The pharmacist," my grandfather was told by the neighbors, "has a special glass apparatus for checking all kinds of liquors. Let him examine the bottle, and we'll know if it's brandy or grape wine."

My grandfather took the liquor, brought it to the pharmacy, and poured the pharmacist a cup, holding the bottle carefully so that it shouldn't even graze him, since one touch from a Gentile was enough to ruin good wine. "It's cognac," said the pharmacist after testing it. As no one in our town knew what cognac was, he explained that it was a special sort of brandy, and that the kind in my grandfather's bottle was so rare that a single drop of it cost more

than all the bottles in a Jewish grog shop. "In that case,"
said my grandfather, "there's no doubt that this is brandy
left over from the Passover." He tucked the bottle in his
coat and started out for the river to get rid of it there. By
then, though, half the town had gathered in front of the
pharmacy. Everyone knew that the Viennese professor's
gifts were special ones, and that the drink that Reb Yehuda
was about to pour out might belong on an emperor's table.
Not everyone in our town was as pious as my grandfather;
not a few Jews were distressed by the thought of the special
liquid being spilled into the Stripa, and pleaded with him to
be given a taste of it first. *Reb Yehuda,* they said in Yiddish,
lozt mikh khotsh a leck tien, let me have a tiny lick of it.
And ever after it was said of would-be sinners in our town
that they only wanted a lick from Reb Yehuda's bottle.

Schwenke entered the office. Herr Lublin glanced at his
watch and remarked: "Schwenke knew that we were about
to go, and came to lock up. You can go too now, Schwenke.
Your wife and children are hungry and are waiting for you
for their supper. Hurry, before your cabbage and potatoes
get cold. I know it's cabbage and potatoes, because that's
what they gave out in the food lines today."

Herr Lublin took the theater tickets, stuck the evening
paper in his pocket, and said, "Let's go." On our way he
took off his hat, passed a hand over his brow, and began to
talk. "You have to realize," he said, "that we knew nothing
about our son except that he had been taken prisoner by
the French. We didn't know if he had been wounded, and if
he had been, how seriously, and whether or not he had
recovered. All we knew, really, was that he was alive. Then
came a notice from the Red Cross that there was a letter
from him. When it arrived, we first read it standing, and
then, again sitting down. It's written in his own hand. In

fact his handwriting is exactly the same as it is on the postcards he used to send to us before the war when he went hiking with his friends all over Germany. Not a single letter of the alphabet is different; we compared the words "I am well" with the same words before the war, and they were identical. If I didn't believe he was forced to write what he wrote, I'd be genuinely puzzled, since we know from our own newspapers how barbaric the enemy is. And even if the papers exaggerate a bit, by how much can it be? They may not even exaggerate at all, since nobody can say that we treat our prisoners like angels of mercy either. Well, here we are at the theater. We may not enjoy the play, but at least we'll enjoy not having to think of the war for a while."

6

We entered the theater and checked our hats and coats with a hat-check girl. The woman gave us a little copper disc with a number on it, and Herr Lublin tipped her handsomely. You might say it was good of him to gladden her poor heart with such a tip, and you might say it wasn't, as it encouraged a certain type of German to complain that the Jews were buying out Germany with their money. After the hat-check girl, came the program seller, and after the program seller, the auditorium. Herr Lublin surveyed the theater with a glance and whispered with satisfaction that there weren't any Nachhuts to be seen. I followed him to seats in the third row center that were regularly reserved for the Lublins whenever they came to see a show. We sat and waited for the curtain to go up.

I was never a theater goer myself, because preparing to go

to the theater always seemed like such fuss. When I could go
without fussing, I went, and if the play wasn't too bad, and
the actors didn't ruin too much, I would even enjoy myself.
Maybe I enjoyed the play I saw with Herr Lublin and maybe
I didn't, but at least there was no fuss or preparing. The
play itself? It was like most modern plays. Different times,
different tastes, different plays: the old ones were no longer
staged and you only saw new ones instead. In place of
sublimity and pathos, you were given reality and truth, and
since not every playwright knew what these were, you were
given what he thought they were. And even if he captured
some truth in his play, this was sure to get lost in the antics
of the actors and actresses. One way or another, the stage
had become a place for mediocrities, who did and said such
ordinary things that you might hear them in any home.
Only the homes you might hear them in were at least real,
whereas those of the theater were cut out of cardboard, so
that it was a wonder they didn't collapse on their
inhabitants.

But I'm generalizing, and I still haven't said a word about
the play I saw with Herr Lublin. Herr Lublin suspected his
wife of having helped the playwright plot it, and even of
having written part of it herself. If she had, though, what
had happened to the charm that was always in her speech,
and why wasn't I drawn to her play as to her? Perhaps the
playwright had rewritten her part of it, or perhaps she was
one of those women who was charming only in person, and
whose graces evaporated as soon as they were set down in
print.

Nothing that begins doesn't end. The play ended too, and
as soon as it did, the applauders and bravoers applauded and
bravoed, some from sheer force of habit, others to show
others what connoisseurs they were. The ovation brought

the author onstage, where he stood looking very military in uniform. He had never been in battle, for he worked in a wartime office that the war had made for itself, but whoever wore soldier's clothes in those days was considered to be a soldier. He and his uniform were bravoed too, and when the actors and actresses saw they were being forgotten, they remembered to come running onstage again themselves. The male and female leads each took the playwright by a hand, while the rest of the cast lined up to their left and right in order of rank and popularity. They bowed and curtsied until the clapping faltered and the applause began to die out. Then they went backstage to take off their make-up and become ordinary people again, the kind that playwrights wrote about in their plays.

"If you're hungry," said Herr Lublin as we left the theater, "we can take a cab to Glueckstock's, and if you're not, let's walk. What did you think of the play? If the people who write such stuff are trying to show us model human beings, they can keep their models to themselves. And if they're trying to show us terrible sinners, I admit that they're trying, but where is the sin? Well, I really have no right to judge. I don't get to read many books, and what I read is only to make Nora happy. The newspapers are enough for me. I read the sections that interest me and skip those that don't, like the literature and art and theater pages. Still, that playwright is an idiot. Nora gave him a nice story and he ruined it with his moronic dialogue and poetic kitsch. I know the story, and believe me, even I could hardly recognize it. Nora didn't come because of her close friends and relatives, whom she was afraid would notice that the play was about her. She needn't have worried. She could have trusted the author to have turned everything around even if he understood what she told him. What still seems strange to me, though, is that you'd think he must have read her the script, so that she could have edited it if she wished. Well, maybe the producers had something to do with it. They know what the public wants these days, and that's what they try to give it."

7

We arrived at the restaurant. Glueckstock brought all kinds of fancy dishes to our table and boasted to Herr Lublin that everything was bona fide, not ersatz of ersatz or black market goods. Whatever he served in his restaurant was bought on the up-and-up, no matter what it cost; even if he made no profit on it, even if he had to take a loss, he wanted his customers to be happy.

"It's a pity," said Herr Lublin with a smile, "that not everyone realizes that, so that people deprive themselves of good food and eat the foulest stuff when they could be banqueting at your table. You think I'm teasing you. I'm teasing myself and people like me, who make do with what they're rationed. Do you happen to have any Palestinian wine? I'd like to drink a glass of wine from the country of my friend."

"Do you really come from Palestine?" asked Glueck-stock, looking at me. He shook my hand and wouldn't let it go. Finally he said, "I actually do have a bottle of Palestinian wine, which I've been saving for the day the war ends. But in honor of our guest from Palestine, I'll open it now and drink *l'hayyim* with you."

He opened the bottle and filled three glasses. "So this," he said, looking at me wonderingly, "is what a man from Palestine looks like." He set one glass before Herr Lublin,

another before me, and another before him. "I too was once
engaged to Palestine," he said, lifting his glass, "but the
engagement was called off."

"You'll have to tell us about it," said Herr Lublin.

"I will," said Glueckstock. "When I was young I dreamed
of settling in the Holy Land, of farming its soil and
rebuilding its ruins. And I almost did, in which case I'd have
been sitting today beneath my fig tree and vine, as we
youngsters used to imagine things there from Zionist
speeches and the Hebrew press. It's true that there were
already discouraging rumors about Galician colonists there,
and their difficulties at Mahanayyim, which was founded by
the Tarnow Lovers of Zion Society, but we youngsters were
so romantic, and had such idealistic ideas about the
homeland, that we were sure we wouldn't be affected by all
that. We were naive enough to believe that we'd succeed by
sheer ability and perseverance, and that we'd set an
example for others to come after us, who'd set an example
for still others, and so on.

"Our family had a cousin who was childless. He and his
wife went to live in the Holy Land in the hope of being
blessed with children there. Before that could happen,
though, she died, and our cousin remarried a women who
had children from two previous marriages. They knew he'd
brought money with him from abroad, and they kept after
it until they'd bilked him of every last cent of it. In the end
he returned to Galicia to seek help. 'Our cousin will
probably visit us too,' said my father, 'and we'll hear from
him what's needed for the country, and what you should
take with you, and what's the best way to travel. In fact,
you can even travel with him when he returns to Jerusalem.'
I was already so eager to be on my way that each extra day
seemed a lifetime, but to please my parents I waited for our

cousin to come.

"I sat down and wrote to several of our relatives to ask if our cousin from Palestine had come, and when he planned to visit us. At last we received a postcard from him announcing that, God willing, he hoped to arrive on such-and-such a day. We were all very excited, most of all myself, because he was my ticket to Palestine. The very idea of seeing a Palestinian Jew in the flesh excited me too. There were many Zionists among us, but I had never actually seen anyone from Palestine before.

"One day I was sitting and leafing through some old issues of *Hamagid,* looking for a certain article about colonization in Palestine. Suddenly I heard horses and a carriage outside. I looked out the window and saw a distinguished old man being helped down from the carriage by the coachman, and I knew right away it was him. He was wearing the strangest clothing I'd ever seen, but I took a liking to him and his clothes right away, perhaps because they were likeable, perhaps because they came from Palestine. There was something both measured and quick about him, a combination that lent him a special charm. My mother and father were pleased to have him as our guest, and I was pleased to be able to serve him.

"That night my mother made dinner in his honor, and my father invited some close friends. Not one of them didn't come. Everyone was thrilled to meet a Jew from the Land of Israel, and to hear about it from him. Each guest outdid the others in praise of the Holy Land and of the virtue of living in it. Our cousin sat there beaming; you could tell he was eating it up. Finally the guests turned to him and said, 'And now tell us about it yourself.'

" 'If it's God's promised land that you've been praising,' our cousin began, 'then no praise uttered by mortal man can begin to describe its wonders. But if you're thinking of the country that's being settled by those heretics, who come to be farmers and make its holy soil like any other, then I'm sorry to tell you that it would be better if they never came at all, and didn't pollute the Holy Land with their presence.' And with that he started to tell the nastiest stories about the new colonists, nearly all of whom were degenerate sinners whose one wish was to make goyim of themselves. There wasn't a human fault that he didn't attribute to them. And when he was done taking out his anger on them, he said: 'But the Holy One Blessed Be He has avenged Himself on them, since all their labors have brought them nothing, because the soil of the Holy Land is holy too, and was made by God to yield fruit only to those who observe His laws and commandments.'

"After listening to my cousin, my parents changed their minds about my plans. My father refused to consent to my going, while my mother wept over what might happen to me in a place where even the pettiest offense was enough to bring down God's wrath. I was only flesh-and-blood, after all, and how could I avoid straying now and then, if only in my thoughts, from the straight and narrow path?

"I was terribly depressed. I didn't want to go to Palestine against my parents' will, but neither did I want to live out my life away from it. Just then I came of age to be drafted. Had I left for Palestine already, I wouldn't have had to serve in the army, but now that I hadn't, I had to. The thought that this would make my parents feel guilty was almost enough to make me happy. But when I went for my physical it turned out that my eyes were bad, and so I wasn't taken. That's what's kept me from serving in this war too."

"Now that you've told us how you never got to Palestine," said Herr Lublin, "perhaps you'll also tell us how you got to Leipzig instead."

"How did I get to Leipzig?" said Glueckstock. "I didn't really get here, I was gotten. One doesn't always get where one is going. Call it chance, if you wish, or call it circumstance. One way or another, I'm still amazed at the way things turned out. It's really a long story, and not one story but many, but I'll try to make it as short as I can."

"If the story is as good as this food of yours," said Herr Lublin, "it can be as long as you like. So?"

"So, my father owned a hardware store. One of his customers was a large Jewish landowner who saw how unhappy I was. 'I hear you're in a temper because you didn't get to go to Palestine,' he said to me. 'I hope you don't mind me giving you some advice. I happen to own a big estate with lots of land and many hands to work it. If a fine young fellow like you were to drop in on me one day, I'd invite him for lunch and discuss the world's problems with him, but I'd save the farm work for the Polish farm hands, because they know how to farm. Here you are, wanting to be a farmer in Palestine, when you've never even held a plow, or any other tool, in your life! If you'd like to learn farming, come with me to my village; you can stay with me three or four months, and see what farm work is like, and if it appeals to you, you can even try it yourself. I'll talk to your parents about it, and I'm sure they'll agree. I don't live far from here, and I'm even a distant relative of yours on your mother's side.'

"I went with him to his village and lived in his house. My first day there I went out to the fields and started to hoe. In no time my hands were all blisters, which took several days to go away. As soon as they did I went back to work, but this time I was careful not to overdo it. I'd work a little and rest some, work a little more and rest even more. The landowner consoled me that in the course of time I'd get used to it until I'd be able to keep up with any peasant.

"When I wasn't out in the fields, I'd look at the books that belonged to the landowner's daughter. Most of them were in Polish, and a few in German; there wasn't a Hebrew or a Yiddish book among them. Once I said to her 'You know, you amaze me: a Jewish girl like you who never has tried to learn her own language and literature!' She thought it over and said, 'You're the first person ever to say that to me. Now that I think about it, you're probably right, but what can I do? Before one learns a language, one has to know the alphabet, and I don't even know what a Hebrew or a Yiddish letter looks like.' She was so innocent that she didn't know that the Hebrew and Yiddish alphabets were the same. To make a long story short, I offered to teach her to read Hebrew, which pleased her parents no end. She wasn't a very good student, and I saw at once that she'd make no rabbi a wife, but in the end she made me one, because after a few weeks of studying together, or pleasantly chatting, we went to her mother and father and asked their blessing to get married. They pretended to be surprised, and we pretended to believe them, as we did with my own parents, who in the meantime had gotten wind of it too. . . . But you must be wondering, Herr Lublin, what my not getting to Palestine, and my getting to a Galician village instead, have to do with my getting to Leipzig."

"Why bother to ask?" said Herr Lublin. "Sooner or later I'm sure you'll get to it yourself."

"Before I do," said Glueckstock, "let's have another glass of wine and drink another *l'hayyim*. Here's to your health, Herr Lublin, and to yours, my Palestinian friend. There's something about your face that reminds me of our cousin

from there. Not that he really looked like you — and you
certainly aren't dressed like him, and don't have his side
curls and beard. Well, anyway, how did I get to Leipzig? It
happened like this.

"My mother-in-law had a younger brother who went into
business for himself as a young man. He used to buy chickens
and eggs and resell them to retailers in Germany. After a
few visits there he found himself a wife and settled in
Dortmund. He was too engrossed in his own affairs to
attend his niece's, that is, my wife's wedding, but to make
up for it he invited us to spend our honeymoon with him.
After the seven days of the wedding week, we left for
Dortmund. I liked Germany right away. One day my wife's
uncle asked her what she thought of the country. 'What
difference does it make what we think of it,' I answered for
her, 'if we have to go back to Galicia in the end?' 'What
makes you think you have to go back?' asked my wife's
uncle. 'Stay here as long as you like, and I'll find work
for you to earn a living.' My wife was of one mind with me.
Before long my uncle took me into his business, where I
spent several years. Then he died young, and his sons sold
the business without taking me into account. My wife and I
tried one thing after another, until I'd lost whatever savings
I'd managed to put away during the years I worked for my
uncle. One day I came to Leipzig to look into a partnership
I'd been offered by a Galician butter-and-cheese importer. It
so happened that I stepped into a restaurant on Pfaffen-
dorfer Street to eat. The owner began to talk with me and
we struck up a friendship. A few days later he said to me as
I was paying the bill, 'It doesn't look to me like you're
about to leave Leipzig so soon, which means that I'll see
you here in my restaurant again. Let's settle the bill when
you leave.' I liked the idea and I didn't. I liked it because

my money was running low and I didn't want to be left with an empty pocket, but I didn't like it because I would have to pay up in the end, and what was I going to do then?

"A few days later he said to me, 'I see you're cutting down on your meals. If you're worried about money, your credit is good, and you can pay me when you get back to Galicia. There's no hurry about it, either. I'm not a young man, but I trust God to let me live a while longer. You can pay your debt whenever you want.'

"Eventually I came to the realization that there was nothing for me in Leipzig. Whatever business offers I'd gotten were either not to my liking or demanded an investment that I didn't have. One day I told the restaurant owner that I was leaving the next morning. Why? I told him that too. 'If I understand your situation,' he said, 'gold coins aren't cooking in gravy where you come from either. If you'd like, why don't you come work for me, either keeping my books or running my kitchen? Until you find something better for yourself, you can earn a decent living right here.'

"When I wrote my wife about it, she sent back a letter full of tears. She'd been raised in a home where Jews were always dropping in to eat and drink without ever paying for their food, and were even given an extra something for the road — and now I wanted her to serve food for a living and count every slice of bread and spoonful of gravy eaten by her customers in order to charge them for it! I wrote back that unfortunately we could no longer return to her parents' home, as her mother was dead and her father was remarried to a woman who didn't even want him around, and that we could no longer return to my parents either, because there was no room for our children there. Whatever offers I'd gotten were either no good or unacceptable for one reason

or another, so now that I'd finally been offered a job that
didn't demand an investment, it seemed unwise to refuse.
My wife wrote back that I should do what I had to, and that
she would stand by me all the way. And that, Herr Lublin,
is how I came to live in Leipzig. There's more to it than
that, but at least I've told you the main part. I see that
there's still a little wine left in the bottle. Let's split it
among us, and drink *l'hayyim* once more, and thank
whoever is responsible for our good luck."

8

Herr Lublin's mood mellowed from all the good food and
drink we had at Glueckstock's, and he began to talk. At first
it was about nothing special, then about things that are
talked about only between friends, and then about his wife
and family. I was not a little taken aback by his confi-
dences, but once I'd gotten over my surprise I listened
intently. Since the day I came to know Herr Lublin he had
never spoken to me like this, nor would it have occurred to
me that he could be so candid about his private thoughts.

Over two hundred years ago, I mused, a certain learned
rabbi from Poland had come to Berlin to expound Jewish
learning and Torah; he wrote several well-known books
there as well, after one of which, *Netsach Yisra'el,* he came
to be known as Rabbi Yisra'el Netsach. As an old man he
returned to Poland and died there; I once even visited his
grave. The great rabbi Nateh Netsach, who was born in our
town, was one of his descendants and as a child I knew
several old scholars who still remembered him. Herr Arno
Lublin, with whom I was now walking in Leipzig while he
told me about his life both before and after leaving our

town, was a descendant of Nateh Netsach's. What remained in him of his forefathers? Certainly not learning, nor piety, nor Jewishness. He didn't even look like a Jew. He was tall, with clear, blue eyes, and had a clipped way of speaking and doing things that bespoke authority. Where had he gotten it from? As nothing in his biography helped explain it, he must have inherited it. Yet while I knew nothing about Rabbi Yisra'el Netsach's height, Arno Lublin's own parents, so I'd heard, were short. I knew nothing about his ancestors' eyes either, though generally, when I thought of wise Jews, I pictured them with brown eyes, while Arno Lublin's were blue. Perhaps he had gotten them from his mother.

I'll relate, then, some of what Herr Lublin said to me while we were walking off our meal. I don't remember his exact words, but I'll try to recapture them because I liked the way he talked, which had a beginning, a middle, and an end, unlike the speech of most of our townsmen, who preferred sounding deep to being clear, so that they spoke in half-sentences and enigmas that you were expected to pretend to understand. Herr Lublin, though he was raised in our town, spoke plainly and to the point, like a merchant laying out his wares before a customer. And as his remarks about his family were the most personally revealing to me, I'll confine myself to them, or at least to what I remember of them, and of the manner in which he said them. The beginning, middle, and end may be missing too, but the gist of them, I hope, remains.

"Perhaps I would never have married my wife," said Herr Lublin, "because I was a small town boy and she was a big city girl. I was raised in grinding poverty, and she in wealth and comfort. I don't know if I ever told you, but she was the daughter of the same man whose luggage I carried home for him that time from the railroad station. He gave me his son's old clothes to wear, and took me into his business, and put me in charge of his staff, and was never anything but kind to me, so that whatever I am today is because of him. And yet I must say that he never so much as hinted to me in passing that I owed my wealth and happiness to him. And the same was true of his sons and my wife. My wife and I don't see eye-to-eye on everything, but one thing we've always agreed on is that she's the boss in the house. And that's included the raising of our children as well. Not that she's any wiser than me, but she always took it so for granted that the house and the children were hers that it was easy for me to give in and let her have her way. A man can be his own master everywhere but in his own home.

"It's a terrible thing to have a son in a prison camp," said Herr Lublin. "To tell you the truth, though, as long as my boy is a prisoner of the enemy's I can at least rest assured that he won't be taken prisoner by . . . well, by the daughter of that ex-prima donna, for example. When I think of Lemke and I being in-laws, and of that daughter of his calling me Papa, my blood begins to boil. A father can't help loving his son, and I certainly love mine, and wish him happiness, but if happiness for him means that *shiksa,* let him stay a prisoner in France.

"I don't know," said Herr Lublin, "who that scholar whose descendant you say I am is. You say he taught Mendelssohn philosophy, and I don't know what that is either. But there's one thing I do know, and that's my own son. He's a good boy, and he deserves the best from life, and I can only hope and pray that he comes home soon safe and sound, and that he marries a good girl from a decent family, and forgets this nonsense about sports and the university, and comes into my business with me, and learns to do an honest day's work. My oldest boy wants no part of business.

If he wants to be a lawyer, I won't stand in his way, though you can't tell me that an honest businessman isn't a cut above a lawyer, who's obliged by his work to defend all kinds of criminals and frauds.

"Once," said Herr Lublin, "when I used to see sensible fathers, who knew that Zionism was a pipedream, let their sons become Zionists anyway without so much as saying boo, I couldn't believe it. Now that my youngest boy's grown up, let me tell you, Zionism may be a pipe-dream, but at least it keeps them from assimilation. There was a time when I couldn't understand why men who have given their lives to Germany, and who had helped through their businesses to extend German interests all over the world, should mind their sons leaving the fold. What was still Jewish about *them* that they should care so much about their children? Now that I look at my wife's family, though, I can see that it's not their sons leaving that bothers them, it's the *shiksas* they bring back with them. Last New Year's Eve I was at a party at some cousin of Nora's and the house was full of young folk, among them a Gentile girl that this cousin's youngest son had married. I'm no expert on women, but believe me, the ugliest old maid in Galicia whose father's beard comes down to his knees is prettier, not to say smarter. So there's Nora's cousin sitting in this wheel-chair of his with a cigar in his hand, which he puts down to reach into his pocket and take out a little box that he gives to the *shiksa.* You should have seen her eyes pop out of her head when she opened it and saw the diamond glittering there. So she bends over to kiss her father-in-law, and do you know what she says? 'Give us your bald spot, you old darling,' she says, 'I want to give it a smackeroo.'

"I've given up all hope for the Jews," said Herr Lublin to me. "I pay my congregational dues. I give when someone

asks for a contribution to a Jewish charity, and once or
twice on the high holy days I even go to the temple. If
anything, the war has made me a little more optimistic,
because now that the Germans have seen how we Jewish
citizens have given to a man of our sons and money to the
war effort, it's inconceivable that they'll still want to
discriminate against us in the future, isn't it? But why are
you looking at me?"

"I didn't know that I was," I said. "Since you mention it,
though, I'll try my best not to do it again."

"I certainly didn't mean to forbid you to look at me,"
laughed Herr Lublin. "Look we're practically home."

If it weren't for my dislike of symbolistic pretences, I
would have said to him, "I'm afraid you're wrong, Herr
Lublin." As it was, I wished him good night, and went on
thinking about him and myself on my way back to my
room. And what I thought about him on that Leipzig street
that night, after he'd confided to me things that most men
don't confide even to themselves, was this:

What was it about Herr Lublin that had drawn me to him
more than to anyone else in Leipzig? It wasn't his help in
getting me a resident's permit, because such favors are easily
forgotten. And it wasn't that we came from the same town
either, because there were other townsmen of mine in
Leipzig whom I didn't befriend. What it was, I thought, was
the sheer novelty of him, because I had never before met
anyone from our town who had put it so completely behind
him, so that even when he remembered it, he remembered it
unkindly.

And what had drawn Herr Lublin to me? Certainly not
my being his townsman either, because he wasn't friendly
with anyone else from our town in Leipzig. "You know,"
said Herr Lublin, "my father was such a terrible miser that I

don't think there was ever another like him. He wouldn't buy a thing for the house that wasn't absolutely necessary for physical survival. It was a concession on his part to sweeten his tea with licorice root, and even that he did grudgingly. Once before the Passover your grandfather came to buy some salt from him. My father dealt in salt — that was all he dealt in, in fact — and the most pious Jews would buy their Passover salt only from him. Your grandfather bought half a sack of salt and began looking about for a porter to carry it back to his house. 'You good-for-nothing!' my father shouted at me. 'Why are you standing there like a pillar of salt yourself? Take the sack and bring it to Reb Yehuda's house.' So I took it and brought it to your grandfather's house. In payment your grandfather gave me a lump of sugar. I had never tasted sugar before in my life. I turned it this way and that, until suddenly it was in my mouth. I can still remember how astonished I was at the way it melted there and how good it made me feel. Your grandfather noticed and gave me a whole handful of it. Whenever I think of our town," said Herr Lublin, "I get a salty taste in my mouth. If it weren't for your grandfather's sugar, I'd never get rid of it."

9

I returned to my room and prepared myself for bed. After my talk with Herr Lublin, and the evening before with its theater, its restaurant, its wine, and its encounter with Lise Lotte Lemke, I was exhausted and wanted to sleep.

There was a sound of horses outside. This amazed me, because all the horses had been commandeered at the outset of the war and not one had been left in the city. I went to the window and saw three handsome steeds with their riders. A fourth, white horse stood beside them.

I laughed and thought, what a pity I'm not sleeping, since if I were it would be a good sign, because it says in the talmudic tractate of *Berakhot,* p. 56b, that whoever sees a white horse in his dream, be it standing or galloping, is in luck.

In no time the horses had drawn up in front of the building where I lived. The riders dismounted, hitched their mounts to a telephone pole, and exchanged a few words. They spoke in a strange language I had never heard before. Here and there a word sounded like the bits of French in the medieval commentaries of Rashi, or like the German in the works of the early Ashkenazi pietists. The manner of speaking was harsh, though, and seemed out-of-tune. I couldn't even guess what tongue it might be, or what country they might come from.

Well, there's a war on, I thought to myself, and it's safest to shut one's eyes and see nothing. Who knows that tomorrow I won't be called before a military court for consorting with these men? I stepped back from the window and passed a hand over my eyes.

"This must be it," I heard one of the riders say. "He's here. According to the directions we were given, this is his house. Look, I see a light on up there."

How did I understand what he said? A better question might have been whom the three horsemen were looking for in my building, since as usual, I knew nothing about my neighbors. Indeed, I was a man who would sooner have moved to another room than have befriended a neighbor, because though I have nothing against people in general, I hated the thought of someone who might drop in on you at any hour of the day or night. Now, though, I was sorry about it, because I'd have given a great deal to know who lived in the building beside me, and especially, whom the three foreign riders were looking for in the dead of night. And yet I didn't stay by the window to find out. There was a war on, and some questions were better unasked.

Just then I heard footsteps that shook the stairs of the house. Someone was stomping up them. I heard doors and windows opening. "Who's making that racket out there?" voices called out. "The nerve of waking up people in the middle of the night! It's time to sleep now, not to play games on the stairs!" There were more shouts, which were interrupted by a man's wild cursing:

"You can all go to hell, you Saxons! You're a gang of traitors, you are! Why don't you stick your tongues up your asses and shut up? We're envoys from the emperor. You'd better tell us what we want to know."

The shouts died down all at once. There was a sudden hush. The tenants were so quiet that you could hear their eyelashes rattling with terror. Their fear infected me too.

"Which room is —'s?" asked one of the three riders. Since I knew he couldn't be asking about me, I assumed I had only imagined it in my confusion, for what could the emperor's envoys want with me? I tried to make myself as small as I could, for three reasons. The first reason was that if I seemed small to myself, I'd know for sure that the emperor's riders couldn't be looking for me. The second reason was that even if they were, they wouldn't be able to find me. The third reason was that even if they found me, I'd seem so unimportant to them that they would leave me alone.

There was a knock on the door of my room. The landlady entered in a nightgown and said in a deathly frail voice:

"Please, there are three important gentlemen riders who would like to see you, please."

"Who would like to see me?" I repeated.

"Yes," she answered, "who would like to see you. They're from the emperor. Here, I've brought you a coat to put on."

I looked at her in astonishment. She had never spoken to me so gently or respectfully before.

The words weren't out of her mouth when the three horsemen barged in. They were wearing outfits so strange that even my dissertation on clothes wouldn't have mentioned them. Two of them had black hair and beards, while the third, who twirled his mustache with his left hand, was blond with a beard full of curls. If his cheeks and forehead hadn't been scarred by the pox, he would have been strikingly handsome. All three were lean and of average height, though it looked to be greater than average.

My room was not large. I, who knew how to make myself small, somehow fit into it; they, who were used to seeming bigger than they were, did not. I needn't bother to explain how difficult it was to entertain under such circumstances.

"Perhaps," whispered the landlady to me, "you'd do me the honor of bringing your guests to my drawing room."

"What are you whispering there, you Saxon wench?" asked one of the riders. Another stuck his right foot between her legs and hoisted her up to the ceiling, where she banged her head and screamed. All three shook with laughter.

"Why are you screaming?" asked one.

"She isn't," said another, "it's the lice in her hair."

They roared with laughter again.

"Bring us some wine, and make it snappy," said a rider.

"Don't you hear well?" said a second.

The landlady went out and returned with a large pitcher of beer. One of the horsemen took it and said:

"Now what about my friends?"

"I'll bring glasses for all of you," stammered the landlady.

"You needn't bother for a few damned drops," laughed the horsman, emptying the pitcher in one quaff.

The landlady stood there at a loss.

"Go ask the neighbors for more," I said to her. "The bill is on me."

She went out and returned with two more pitchers of beer. They drank, wiped their mouths, and drank again. "And what about you?" they asked, looking at me. "We haven't seen you drink anything yet."

"I've already had wine and some cognac," I said.

"Wine?" said one. "If there's wine around, why are we drinking beer?"

"You mentioned another drink," said his friend. "Say it again.'

"Cognac?" I said.

"What? What's that? Ko-ko-ac? Is that what they drink in that country of yours?"

"As a matter of fact," I said, "they do make it in Palestine nowadays. But people generally prefer wine there."

"And to think we thought that everyone in the Holy Land drank Jordan water!"

"The way I heard it," said a horseman, "the people drink Jordan water, and the lords and bishops drink wine."

When they had finished their beer, one asked:

"You mentioned another drink. How does it taste, and what do you call it?"

"I can tell you what we call it," I answered, "but not how it tastes."

"Do you drink it from a goblet or a pitcher?" he asked. I told him.

"When our emperor makes war on the Holy Land," he

said, "you'll see how I'll drink a whole pitcher of it without even stopping for breath."

"Our emperor won't make war on the Holy Land," said his friend, "because our Emperor Charles and the emperor of the Holy Land are at peace. Didn't you hear that the emperor of the Holy Land sent our emperor the key to the Holy Sepulchre as a gift?"

"And what if he did? Don't you suppose our emperor's ministers have brains enough to find a good reason to make war on him anyway?"

"You, my friend and chevalier," said the first horseman, "are a great numbskull for talking like that in front of these Saxons, who are traitors every one of them. Wench, who gave you permission to stay here and listen to us?"

He threw his pitcher of beer at the landlady's feet. She took fright and ran out of the room.

"We've come from the emperor," said the leader of the riders when she'd left. "The Emperor Charles has sent for you."

I recalled that Franz Josef, Emperor of Austria and Hungary, had recently died, and that the crown had passed to his son Charles. It saddened me to think of Franz Josef, though he'd lived to a ripe old age, because he had been a good king to the Jews and there had been peace in his time. Now that he was gone, God only knew what lay in store for us, and what his son Charles would do in his place, for even if he was no anti-Semite himself, he was bound in the hands of his ministers and advisers. I still hadn't realized that it wasn't Charles, King of Austria, who had sent for me, but Charlemagne, King of the Franks.

They put me on the spare horse and off we rode, the mounts gnashing at their bridles as they flew. We passed through towns and villages, forests and ruins. Darkness

descended and no man was seen on the roads, for
Charlemagne had put the Saxons to the sword and razed all
their homes, so that whoever still had the breath of life in
him hid from the emperor's wrath. Of all the peoples of the
earth, Charlemagne hated none like the Saxons; eight times
he had already ridden through their lands wreaking havoc,
yet still the carnage was not done.

We rode on and on, passing many places. On our way the
emperor's envoys, who rode on either side of me, told me
many interesting things, especially the curly-bearded blond
one, who had been in the emperor's retinue when
Charlemagne journeyed to Rome to receive an accounting
from the Pope of all his sins, of which many great Christians
and high clerics had told him. Once even, when the Pope
was riding through Rome on a she-mule, he was dragged
from it by the mob, which trampled and blinded him, and
tore out his tongue. The story so astounded me that I forgot
to ask my companion about Charlemagne's coronation by
the Pope, and whether this had happened before the Pope's
blinding or after. The blond horseman also told me of a gift
the Pope sent to Charlemagne, a shroud full of saints' bones,
which the emperor was exceedingly fond of; in fact, he was
inseparable from them, especially from one bone which,
according to Roman priestly tradition, belonged to a martyr
who had been flayed alive by pagans, and who hadn't wept
or uttered a groan, but on the contrary, had beamed
joyfully as though he were being anointed with myrrh, and
before giving up the ghost had said six words in the Hebrew
tongue, which were the very same words Jews said before
their death, especially when they were being slaughtered for
refusing to become Christians.

I heard many more things from the emperor's envoys too,
some of them simple, others so confused that they seemed

to belong to a dream. To pass the time, I occupied myself
by wondering what would be my case in Jewish law if I
were a member of the priestly caste who was forbidden to
come in contact with the dead: could I or couldn't I enter
the emperor's pavilion, in which there were human bones,
and not only bones, but the bones of a saint who had cried
six words in the Hebrew tongue at the time of his death,
which must have been the prayer "Hear, O Israel," which
meant that he was a Jew by birth, in which case his bones
were still Jewish despite his becoming a Christian? On the
third day of riding we reached the emperor's camp.

I was ushered into the emperor's pavilion.

The emperor was a pious Christian, and he wore the
symbol of his faith around his neck. I sought to spiritualize
my thoughts, and I recited the blessing "Who has given of
His grandeur to a king of flesh-and-blood," as a Jew is
enjoined to do, being careful not to bow or bend my head,
God forbid, before a mere human being. I was grateful to
the Pope for having crowned Charlemagne as emperor,
which meant I could address him as "My sire the emperor"
rather than "my sire the king," for there was no king but
the King of Kings, the Holy One Blessed Be He.

The emperor's servants brought several large stones and
piled them by the emperor's seat. The minister of state
spread a woolen rug over them and whispered to me, "The
emperor bids you be seated. Sit here."

I sat and waited for Charles or one of his ministers to
speak.

"Where is the goose for writing?" asked the emperor.

The words weren't out of his mouth when a servant came
bearing a large plump goose. If it wasn't descended from the
legendary goose of Rabba Bar Bar Hanna, it was an even
greater wonder than that where such a plump goose might

have come from. The emperor regarded it amiably and ran his right hand over its feathers before seizing two or three of them and plucking them out. The goose screeched terribly, while the emperor and his court screamed with laughter. Then the ministers watched silently while a pot of ink and some parchment were brought in on a golden tray.

"We have heard," said the emperor, "that you know the tongue of the Hebrews, and can write in it too."

I nodded and said, "I am a Hebrew myself, and I know my ancestors' tongue, nor is the manner of its writing beyond my ken."

He laughed till his sides split, then ordered the goose removed from the tent.

"Shall I have it roasted for your dinner?" asked the servant.

" 's blood!" the emperor rebuked him. "Roast me for my dinner the deer I shot today, and make sure it's how I like it."

"But Sire," said a minister, pressing his hand to his heart, "you know that the physician has told you that deer meat isn't good for you."

"Next you'll tell me," laughed the emperor, "that the physician wishes me to eat dove meat like a woman with child. Go roast me my deer as I've asked you."

The servant left with the goose. The emperor gave the feathers to a minister and said, "Take these quills and prepare them for writing."

The minister took them and sharpened them with a sword that he drew from its sheath.

"Is everything ready for writing?" asked Charlemagne.

"Yes, Sire," said the minister.

"And you," Charlemagne asked me, "are you ready too?"

I sat as one speechless, for I knew not what it was about.

"I can see," said the emperor angrily, "that no one has told the Jew a thing. Now I shall have to tell him myself, from beginning to end."

"With your kind permission, Sire," said a minister, bowing to the emperor, "I'll tell him what it is that we desire."

The emperor regarded him coldly and said, "Now that I'm here, I can tell him myself without help from such as you." He turned to me and continued: "Listen to why we have called you. You must have heard that the emperor of the Mohametans has sent me an elephant by the person of Isaac the Jew, which gift I'm most pleased with, for never has a Christian king seen so monstrous and wise a beast. And since I value it greatly, I wish to ask Isaac how we may gladden its heart, and what we may add to the provender that it receives each day. And since we know that you can write the same tongue of the Hebrews as can Isaac the Jew, we desire you to pen him a letter exactly as we tell you."

What a pity, I thought to myself, that I wasn't sleeping, for if I were I might see the elephant in my dreams, and the Talmud said that whoever saw an elephant in his dreams was a candidate for wonders. Indeed, had the king of the Ishmaelites sent the emperor of the Christians two or three dream elephants, I might have seen wonders of wonders, for it is said, "Unto him who sees an elephant in his dream are done wonders, unto him who sees many elephants, wonders of wonders."

The quills, ink and parchment were brought to me. I sat with my eyes on the emperor.

"Are you ready?" asked Charlemagne.

"I am," I said.

"Well, then," he ordered, "write."

I sat and wrote, "From Charles, King of all the Franks, to Isaac the Jew, who sits before the emperor of the Saracens, peace and fond greetings."

"Have you written that?"

"I have."

"Well, write on. 'Whereas we have consented to receive from the emperor of the Saracens his munificent gift, a monstrous beast which brings great cheer to us and our servants, whom we have graciously permitted to look upon it, and whereas we desire to gladden its heart in requital for its company, we have determined to ask you how we may do so, and what may be a cause of satisfaction to it.' Have you written all that?"

"Every word."

"And does the quill still obey you? Or shall I have another goose brought to make new ones?"

I felt sorry for the geese, and asked the emperor not to send for more. Indeed, I had a miracle pen with me, only I was afraid he might think it black magic, for as enlightened an emperor as he was, whatever surpassed his understanding seemed magical to him, and if not to him, then to his counselors and ministers, and most certainly, to his bishops.

The emperor suddenly reached out and seized the letter. He studied it once, and then again, as though he couldn't look at it enough. "Is it not most marvelous?" he said to his ministers and counselors. "A man sits here in Thueringen and writes a letter to Babylonia or Persia. They are indeed a wise people, the Jews, if they can write their own tongue like this."

"But you too, Sire, know how to write," said one of the ministers with a bow.

"In sooth," said the emperor, "I can write the letters of my name. Hand me your quill and one of your parchments, and I'll show you."

I handed him the quill and a parchment.

He flourished the quill and began to write his own name, while all his ministers crowded around him and marveled at the sight of an emperor writing like a scribe.

"There," said Charlemagne, putting down the quill and regarding what he had written. "I've done most of it. The rest we can leave for tomorrow. Now bring me a cup of the drink we received from the Bishop of Mainz and his wife, that I and my guest may quaff of it."

I tried to think what to do. Did I have the strength of character to tell the emperor that I couldn't drink his wine with him?

"If God has given you a proper tongue to taste with," said the emperor to me, "drink this and tell me if it is not truly a wonder of wonders. The Bishop of Mainz has sent me a berry juice that tastes like the choicest of wines."

"The Lord is good to all," I thought in the words of the Psalmist, "His mercy is over all His handiwork." And I whispered to myself: "Blessed be He who has saved me from the sin of drinking the wine of Gentiles."

A cup was poured me, and I said the blessing for fruit juice over it.

"Is that which you said over your cup in the tongue of the Hebrews too?" asked the emperor.

I nodded.

"And is that," he asked, "the same tongue spoken by our lord David King of Israel?"

I told him that it was.

"But he wrote his psalms in Latin," said the emperor.

"God forbid," I said. "He wrote them in the holy tongue too."

"Have you met our lord David in person?" asked

Charlemagne. "Tell me about him."

I thought it might be impolitic to disillusion the emperor, so I ignored his question, and I told him some stories about David from the Talmud and the Midrash instead.

Charlemagne was so moved by them that he shut his eyes and dozed off. When his ministers saw he was sleeping, they signaled me to stand. I rose and left.

Dawn had broken and a new day had arrived. It's time for the morning prayer, I thought. If I pray here in the emperor's camp, his ministers and serfs will disturb me. I'd better return to Leipzig and pray in my usual place.

I walked back to Leipzig. When I reached the city, I found my room neatly arranged. There wasn't a trace of the events of the other night, when the emperor's envoys were rowdy over their beer.

                              10

Schwenke entered the store with a messenger boy from the municipality bearing a note to me from Herr Lublin, which said more or less:

> It looks as though I'll be kept here a while, and won't get back to the store. Take the cane, give a rap on Lemke's window, and tell him to tell Schwenke to lock up. I couldn't call you because I unplugged the telephone before going out so that you wouldn't be bothered by calls, and now that I needed to phone, I wasn't able to.

I tipped the messenger boy and told him that would be all. Schwenke asked me if I needed anything. I was about to tell him that he should lock up after me when the thought occurred to me, why leave? I wasn't hungry, I didn't feel

like going to the bathhouse, and there wasn't anything else
that I needed to do, while in Herr Lublin's store it was quiet
and there was no one to disturb me. I decided to stay put
until the Sabbath. True, I hadn't prepared any food for my
Sabbath meals, but in any case, it was too late to go
shopping in the marketplace or stores. No doubt I would
find food in my room, and if I didn't, a few hours of
seclusion were well worth having nothing to eat.

I glanced up and saw that Schwenke was still standing
there, as he did before Herr Lublin. I looked at him as Herr
Lublin did and said, "I think I'll stay a while longer."
"Would you like me to fetch you some coffee, Sir?" he
asked. I remembered how he'd brought me coffee once
before, that first evening I'd sat with Herr Lublin in his
store. "No, thank you," I said, shaking my head, "Perhaps
something to eat then, Sir?" he asked. "I really don't want
anything," I said. Schwenke saw that I wished to be alone
and left.

I sat in the store, thinking of what Herr Lublin had told
me and of what I knew about his ancestors. And as
sometimes happens, I forgot for a moment that I was in
Leipzig and imagined I was back in my native town, in its
study hall and streets, stopping to chat with whomever I
met about the old days, which though far from perfect were
a sight better than what came after. It wasn't to do Herr
Lublin a favor that I stayed in his store, but because it felt
good to sit there thinking of where I was raised. It was as
though the four winds had blown a setting of it at my feet,
wall by wall, so real that I nearly rose to go walking in it, as
I used to once walk in my town.

I was dumbstruck by the wonder of it: A man sits in a
hardware store in the middle of Leipzig thinking of his
town, and suddenly, as though by magic, its streets, yards,

markets and houses are transported before him, right in front of his nose! If I didn't have such a low opinion of myself, I'd have thought that the heavens were putting on a special show in my behalf. As such conceits led to vanity, however, I told myself I was dreaming. I opened my eyes to drive off the mirage and saw that I was alone in Herr Lublin's store, Herr Lublin having gone off on some business and left me there by myself.

Translated by Hillel Halkin

Badenheim 1939

AHARON APPELFELD

1

Spring returned to Badenheim. Bells rang in the nearby
country church. The shadows of the forest drew back into
the forest. The sun scattered the remaining darkness, and its
light spilled out along the main street, from square to
square. It was a movement of transition. Soon the holiday-
makers would invade the town. Two inspectors passed from
street to street, checking the flow of sewage in the drains.
Over the years, the town had seen many tenants come and
go but its modest beauty was still intact.

Trudy, the pharmacist's ailing wife, stood at the window.
She looked about her with the feeble gaze of a chronic
invalid. The beneficent sunlight touched her pallid face and
she smiled. A difficult winter, a strange winter, had ended.
Storms played havoc with the housetops. Rumors spread.
Trudy's sleep was disturbed by hallucinations. She spoke
incessantly of her married daughter, while Martin assured
her that everything was all right. That was how the wintᵉ
passed. Now she stood at the window, resurrected.

The low, well-kept houses looked tranquil once again.
Islands of white in a green sea. This is the season when you
hear nothing but the rustle of things growing and then, by

chance, you catch sight of an old man holding a pair of pruning shears, with the look of a hungry raven.

"Has the mail come?" asked Trudy.

"It's Monday today. The mail won't arrive until afternoon."

The carriage of Dr. Pappenheim the impresario charged out of the forest and came to a halt on the main street. Dr. Pappenheim alighted and waved in greeting. No one responded. The street was steeped in silence.

"Who's here?" asked Trudy.

Dr. Pappenheim brings with him the moist breath of the big city, and air of celebration and anxiety. He'll be spending his time at the post office — sending off cables and special delivery letters.

Apart from Dr. Pappenheim's appearance in town, nothing has happened. The mild spring sunshine shone as it does every year. People met at the café in the afternoon, and devoured pink ice-cream.

"Has the mail arrived yet?" she asked again.

"Yes. There's nothing for us."

"Nothing." Her voice sounded ill.

Trudy got back into bed, feverish. Martin removed his jacket and sat down next to her: "Don't worry. We had a letter just last week. Everything is all right." Her hallucinations persisted: "Why does he beat her?"

"No one beats her. Leopold is a very nice man, and he loves her. Why do you think such things?"

Trudy shut up as though she had been scolded. Martin was tired. He put his head on the pillow and fell asleep.

The first of the vacationers arrived on the following day. The pastry shop window was decorated with flowers. In the hotel garden Professor Fusshak and his young wife were to be seen, also Dr. Schutz and Frau Zauberbilt — but to

Trudy they looked more like convalescents in a sanatorium than people on vacation.

"Don't you know Professor Fusshalt?" asked Martin.

"They look very pale to me."

"They're from the city," said Martin, trying to mollify her.

Now Martin knew that his wife was very ill. Medicines would be of no use. In her eyes the world was transparent, diseased and poisoned, her married daughter held captive and beaten. Martin tried in vain to convince her. She stopped listening. That night, Martin sat down to write a letter to Helena, his daughter. Spring in Badenheim is delightful, beautiful. The first vacationers are already here. But your mother misses you so.

Trudy's disease was gradually seeping into him. He, too, began to distinguish signs of pallor on people's faces. Everything at home had changed since Helena's marriage. For a year they had tried to dissuade her, but it was no use. She was in love, head over heels, as they say. A hasty marriage took place.

Dark green spring was now ascending from the gardens. Sally and Gert, the local tarts, strolled along the boulevard dressed for the season. The townspeople had tried at one time to throw them out — a prolonged struggle that came to naught. The place had got used to them, as it had grown used to the eccentricities of Dr. Pappenheim, and to the alien summer people who transplanted themselves here like unhealthy roots. The owner of the pastry shop would not let the "ladies" set foot on his premises, thus depriving them of the most delicious cream cakes in the entire world. Boyish Dr. Schutz, who liked Sally, once took some cakes out to the street. When the owner of the shop found out about it later, he made a scandal but that led nowhere either.

"And how are the young ladies?" asked Dr. Pappenheim merrily.

Over the years they had lost their big city haughtiness — they had brought themselves a modest house, and dressed like the local women. There had been a period of riotous parties but the years and the city-bred mistresses had pushed them aside. Were it not for their savings, theirs would have been a sad predicament. They had nothing left but the memories which they mulled over like widows on long winter nights.

"How was it this year?"

"Everything is fine," said Pappenheim cheerfully.

"Wasn't it a strange winter, though?"

They were fond of Pappenheim, and over the years they had become interested in his strange performers. Here, in alien terrain, they grasped eagerly at anything whatsoever.

"Oh don't worry, don't worry — the festival is packed this year — lots of surprises."

"Who will it be this time?"

"A child-prodigy. I discovered him this winter in Vienna."

"A child-prodigy," said Sally maternally.

Next day, the vacationers were all over Badenheim. The hotel bustled. Spring-sunlight and excited people filled the town, and, in the hotel garden, porters hauled the brightly colored luggage. But Dr. Pappenheim seemed to shrink in size. The festival schedule was ruined again. He ran through the streets. For years these performers have been driving him mad, and now they want to wreck him altogether.

After leaving their luggage at the hotel, the people moved on towards the forest. Professor Fusshalt and his young wife were there. A tall man escorted Frau Zauberblit cere-moniously. "Why don't we turn left?" said Frau Zauberblit, and the group did indeed turn to the left. Dr. Schutz lagged behind as though enchanted.

"Why do they walk so slowly?" asked Trudy.

"They're on vacation, after all," said Martin patiently.

"Who is that man walking with Frau Zauberbilt? Isn't that her brother?"

"No, my dear. Her brother is dead. He has been dead for years."

That night the band arrived. Dr. Pappenheim rejoiced as if a miracle had happened. The porters unloaded horns and drums. The musicians stood at the gate like trained birds on a stick. Dr. Pappenheim offered sweets and chocolates. The driver hurried the porters on, and the musicians ate in silence. "Why were you late?" asked Pappenheim, not without relief. "The car was late," they answered.

Dressed in a frock coat, the conductor stood aside, as if all this were no concern of his. He'd had a struggle with Pappenheim the year before. Pappenheim was on the verge of dismissing him, but the senior musicians sided with their conductor, and nothing came of it. The conductor had demanded a contract for the usual three-year period. The quarrel ended in a compromise.

In the past, Pappenheim had lodged them on the ground floor of the hotel, in dark, narrow rooms. There was a clear-cut clause in the new contract providing for proper lodging. Now they were all anxious to see the rooms. Pappenheim walked over to the conductor and whispered in his ear: "The rooms are ready — top floor — large, well ventilated rooms." "Sheets?" asked the conductor. "Sheets as well." Pappenheim kept his promise. They were lovely rooms. Seeing them, the musicians were inspired to change into their blue uniforms. Pappenheim stood quietly by and did not interfere. In one of the rooms a quarrel broke out —

over a bed. The conductor chided them: "Rooms like these
deserve quiet. Now get everything together before you go
down."

At ten o'clock, all was ready. The musicians stood in
groups of three, instruments in hand. Pappenheim was
furious. He would gladly have paid them off and sent them
packing, but he could not afford to. More than anything
else, they reminded him of his failures. Thirty years gone
by. Always late and unrehearsed. Their instruments
produced nothing but noise. And every year, new demands.

The evening began. People swarmed over the band like
hornets. The musicians blew and hammered as though
trying to drive them away. Dr. Pappenheim sat in the back
drinking steadily.

Next day, the place was calm and quiet. Martin got up
early, swept the entrance, wiped the dust off the shelves,
and made out a detailed purchase order. It had been a hard
night. Trudy had not stopped raving. She refused to take
medicine, and finally Martin had tricked her into swallowing
a sleeping mixture.

At approximately ten o'clock, an inspector from the
Sanitation Department entered the pharmacy, and said that
he wanted to look the place over. He asked strange
questions. Ownership title. Had it come through inherit-
ance? When and from whom was it purchased: property
value. Surprised, Martin explained that the place had been
whitewashed and thoroughly disinfected. The inspector
took out a folding yardstick, and measured. Then, neither
thanking him nor apologizing, he went directly out into the
street.

The visit upset Martin. He believed in the authorities, and
therefore he blamed himself. The back entrance was probably not in good enough repair. This short visit spoiled his

morning. There was something in the wind. He went outside
and stood on the lawn. A morning like any other. The
milkman made his rounds bucolically, the musicians
sprawled in the hotel garden sunning themselves, and
Pappenheim left them alone. The conductor sat by himself,
shuffling a deck of cards. In the afternoon, Frau Zauberblit
entered the pharmacy and announced that there is no place
like Badenheim for a vacation. She was wearing a dotted
poplin frock, but to Martin it seemed that her late brother
was about to walk through the door.

"Isn't that strange?" he asked, not knowing what he was
asking.

"Anything can happen," said she as though she had
understood the question.

Martin was angry. It was all because of Trudy.

The musicians stayed in the garden all afternoon. They
looked pathetic out of uniform. For years they had been
used to fighting with Pappenheim, now they fought among
themselves. The conductor did not interfere. He set down
his deck, and watched them. A gaunt musician took a pay
receipt out of his vest pocket, and waved it at his colleagues.
They showed him his mistake. From Martin's garden this
looked like a shadow play, perhaps because the light was
fading. One by one, long shadows unrolled across the green
lawn.

At twilight, the conductor hinted that it might be
advisable to go up and change into uniform. They took their
time, like old soldiers worn out by long service. The
conductor chatted with Pappenheim. For some reason,
Pappenheim found it necessary to give a long-winded
explanation of the festival program. "I hear Mandelbaum is
on the program too. Why, that's a spectacular achievement
— how did you manage it?" "Hard work," said Pappenheim,

and turned to go into the dining room. The guests were
already eating hungrily. The waitress watched the kitchen
door sharply. Her orders were late. But the cynical old
waiters praised the food with an air of self-importance.
Trudy's condition was no better. Martin's endless talk was
futile. Everything seemed transparent and diseased to her.
Helena was a prisoner on Leopold's estate, and when he
comes home from the barracks at night, he beats her.

"But don't you see?" she asked.

"No, I don't see."

"It's only my hallucinations."

Martin was angry. Trudy frequently mentioned her
parents, the little house on the banks of the Vistula. The
parents died and all contact with the brothers was lost.
Martin said that she was still immersed in that world, in the
mountains, with the Jews. And this was, to a certain extent,
the truth. She was tortured by a hidden fear, not her own,
and Martin felt that her delusions were gradually penetrating into him, and that everything was on the verge of
collapse.

2

Next day it was made known that the jurisdiction of the
Department of Sanitation had been extended, and hence-
forth the Department would be entitled to carry out
independent investigations. The modest announcement was
posted on the town bulletin board. Without further ado, the
clerks of the Department set about investigating all places
designated on their map. The detailed investigations were
carried out by means of questionnaires sent in from the
district head office. One of the musicians, who bore his

Polish name with a strange pride, remarked that the clerks reminded him of marionettes. His name was Leon Semitzki. Fifty years ago he had emigrated from Poland with his parents. He had a fondness for his Polish memories, and when in good spirits he would talk about his country. Dr. Pappenheim liked his stories and he would sit with the musicians and listen.

The clouds vanished, and the spring sun shone warmly. A vague anxiety spread over the faces of the old musicians. They sat together and said nothing. Semitzki broke the silence all of a sudden: "I'm homesick for Poland." "Why?" Pappenheim wanted to know. "I don't know," said Semitzki. "I was only seven years old when I left, but it seems like only a year ago."

"They're very poor there," someone whispered.

"Poor, but not afraid of death."

That night, nothing happened in Badenheim. Dr. Pappenheim was melancholic. He could not get Semitzki off his mind. He too recalled those rare visits to Vienna of his grandmother from the Carpathians. She was a big woman, and brought with her the odor of millet, the smell of the forest. Pappenheim's father hated his mother-in-law. Rumors flourished. Some said that the Department was on the track of a sanitary hazard, others thought that this time it might be the Tax Department masquerading as the Sanitation Department. The musicians exchange views. The town itself was calm, cooperative, complying with all the Department's requests. Even the proud owner of the pastry shop agreed to give information. There was nothing noticeably different, but the old musicians surveyed the town, imparting a strange unease.

At the end of April, the two poetry readers showed up. Dr. Pappenehim wore his blue suit in their honor. They were tall and gaunt with an intensely spiritual look. Their passion was Rilke. Dr. Pappenheim, who had discovered them in Vienna seven years before, at once discerned a morbid melody in their voices which enchanted him. Thereafter, he simply could not do without them. At first their readings drew no response, but in recent years people had discovered their elusive melody — and found it intoxicating. Frau Zauberblit sighed with relief: They're here.

The readers were twin brothers who, over the years, had become indistinguishable. But their manner of reading was not the same — as if sickness spoke with two voices; one tender and appeasing, the remains of a voice, the other clear and sharp. Frau Zauberblit declared that without the double voice, life would be meaningless. Their recitals were balm to her, and she would murmur Rilke to herself in the empty nights of spring, as though sipping pure nectar.

The musicians, who worked at dance halls in the winter and resorts in the summer, could not understand what people found in those morbid voices. In vain did Pappenheim try to explain the magic. Only Semitzki said that their voices excited his diseased cells. The conductor hated them — he called them the clowns of the modern age.

And meanwhile spring is at work. Dr. Schutz pines after the schoolgirl like an adolescent. Frau Zauberblit is engrossed in conversation with Semitzki, and Professor Fusshalt's young wife changes into her bathing costume, and goes out to sunbathe on the lawn.

The twins are forever rehearsing. They can't do without the practice. "And I was naive enough to think that it was all spontaneous," said Frau Zauberblit.

"Practising, practising," said Semitzki. "If I had practised when I was young I never would have ended up in this second rate outfit. I wasn't born here. I was born in Poland.

And my parents didn't give me a musical education." After
midnight, Dr. Pappenheim received a cable, worded as
follows: *Mandelbaum taken ill. Will not arrive on time.* Dr.
Pappenheim got up shaking and said: "This is a catastrophe." "Mandelbaum," said Frau Zauberblit. "The entire
arts festival is at stake," said Pappenheim. Semitzki tried to
soothe them, but Pappenheim said, "This is the last straw."
He sank into his grief like a stone. Frau Zauberblit brought
out a bottle of Pappenheim's favorite French wine, but he
wouldn't touch it, and all night long he moaned:
"Mandelbaum, Mandelbaum."

3

And the investigations showed reality for what it was. From
this point on, no one could say that the Department of
Sanitation was ineffective. A feeling of strangeness,
suspicion and mistrust was in the air; still, the residents
went about their usual business. The vacationers had their
pastimes, and the local residents had their worries. Dr.
Pappenheim was inconsolable over his great loss — Mandelbaum. Life was worthless since that cable had arrived.
Professor Fusshalt's young wife declared that something had
changed in Badenheim. The Professor did not leave the
room — his definitive book was about to go to the
publisher, and he was busy with the proofs. His young wife,
whom he spoiled like a kitten, understood nothing about his
books. Her interests were confined to cosmetics and dresses.
At the hotel they called her Mitzi.

In the middle of May, a modest announcement appeared
on the bulletin board, stating that all Jewish citizens must
register with the Sanitation Department before the month
was out.

"That's me," said Semitzki. He seemed to be delighted.

"And me," said Pappenheim. "You wouldn't want to deprive me of my Jewishness, would you?"

"I would," said Semitzki, "But your nose is proof enough that you are no Austrian."

The conductor, who had learned over the years to blame everything on Pappenheim, said: "I have to get caught up in this bureaucratic mess all because of him. The clerks have gone mad, and I'm the one who suffers."

People started avoiding Pappenheim like the plague. He seemed not to notice, and rushed back and forth between the post office and the hotel.

Trudy's condition worsened the last two weeks. She talked on and on about death. No longer out of fear — but rather as if she were coming to know it, preparing to inhabit it. The strong medications that she swallowed drew her from one sleep to the next, and Martin saw her wandering off into the other regions of her life.

People confessed to each other, as if they were talking about a chronic disease which there was no longer any reason to hide. And their reactions varied — pride and shame. Frau Zauberblit avoided talking and asking questions. She pointedly ignored them. Finally she asked Semitzki: "Have you registered?"

"Not yet," said Semitzki. "I'll do it on a more festive occasion. You don't mean to say that I have the honor of addressing an Austrian citizen of Jewish origin?"

"You have indeed, sir."

"In that case, we'll be having a family party in the near future."

"Could you have thought otherwise?"

The sun stopped shining. The headwaiter himself served the white cherries for the cake. The lilac bushes climbed the veranda railing, and bees sucked greedily at the light blue flowers. Frau Zauberblit tied a silk scarf around her straw bonnet. "Brought in from Waldenheim this morning — they ripened early." "That's simply marvelous," said Frau Zauberblit. She adored these local voices.

"What are you thinking about?" asked Semitzki.

"I was remembering my grandfather's house — the rabbi from Kirchenhaus. He was a man of God. I spent my term vacations there. He used to walk along the river in the evenings. He liked growing things." Semitzki did not stop drinking: "Don't worry, children. Soon we'll be on our way — back to Poland."

Dr. Schutz runs about in a stupor. The schoolgirl is driving him mad: "Dr. Schutz, why not join intelligent company for an intelligent conversation?" said Frau Zauberblit. In academic circles, he was considered quite the prodigy — if a bit naughty.

"Have you registered?" said Semitzki.

"What?" he asked in surprise.

"Oh, you have to register, haven't you heard? According to the regulations of the Sanitation Department — which is, of course, a Government Department, a fine Department, a Department whose jurisdiction has been extended these last two months. And this most worthy Department earnestly desires that you, Dr. Schutz, should register."

"This is no laughing matter, my dear," said Frau Zauberblit.

"In that case," he said, confused. He was the pampered darling of Badenheim. Everyone loved him. Dr. Pappenheim lamented his wasted musical talent. The prodigal son of his rich old mother, who never failed to bail him out at the end of the season.

A vague terror lurked in the eyes of the musicians.

"Don't worry," said Dr. Pappenheim, rallying his courage,
though he was feeling melancholy. "But aren't we guests?
Must we sign as well?" asked one of the musicians.

"It is my opinion," said Pappenheim dramatically, "that
the Sanitation Department wishes to boast of its distinguished guests, and will, therefore, enter them in the Golden
Book. Now that is nice of them — don't you think?"

"Maybe its because of the *Ostjuden*," said one of the
musicians.

Semitzki rose to his feet: "What's the matter? You don't
like me? I'm an Eastern Jew through and through — so you
don't like me, eh?"

4

Badenheim's intoxicating spring was causing havoc again.
Dr. Schutz was penniless, and he posted two express letters
to his mother. The schoolgirl, it seems, was costing him a
fortune. Frau Zauberblit and Semitzki sit together all day
long. He might have been the only man left in the world.
Dr. Pappenheim is depressed — the intoxicating spring never
fails to make him sad. Frau Zauberblit already rebuked him:
"I'll defray the losses. Hand me the bill. If Mandelbaum
continues to give you the run around, I'll get the Krauss
chamber ensemble." The twins wander through town
looking cryptic. People at the hotel talk about them in
whispers, as if they were sick. They eat nothing, and only
drink coffee. The headwaiter said: "If only I could serve
Rilke's death sonnets maybe they would eat. That's probably all the food they can digest."

After breakfast, Frau Zauberblit, Semitzki and Pappenheim decided unanimously to register at the Sanitation

Department. The clerk did not so much as raise an eyebrow at Frau Zauberblit's declarations. Frau Zauberblit praised the Department for its order and beauty. No wonder it had been promoted. Semitzki announced that his parents had come from Poland fifty years ago, and that he was still homesick. The clerk wrote all this down without a trace of expression.

That night Semitzki did not wear his blue uniform. The band played. Everyone saw at a glance that Frau Zauberblit had a sweetheart — she glowed like someone in love. The young wife of Professor Fusshalt is going mad. Professor Fusshalt is preoccupied with the book, and he doesn't leave his desk. She's fed up with the people in Badenheim. What is there to do here? Those readings again. They depress her. One of the musicians, a cynic, tried to console her: "Don't be angry. In Poland, everything is beautiful, everything is interesting."

On the following day Trudy's screams were heard in the street. From the hotel veranda, people watched the terrible struggle in progress. No one went down to help. Poor Martin fell on his knees in desperation, and begged: "Trudy, Trudy, be calm. There is no forest here — there are no wolves."

An alien night descended on Badenheim. The cafés were empty, people walked the streets in silence, as though being led along. The town seemed in the grip of some other vacation, from another place. Dr. Schutz led the tall schoolgirl about as though he were going to tie her up. Sally and Gerti strolled arm in arm like schoolgirls. The moist light of spring nights slithered on the pavement. The musicians sat on the veranda, observing the passing flow with sharp looks.

Dr. Pappenheim sat in the corner alone, reckoning sadly: the trio has deserted me again. Nobody will forgive me.

And rightly so. Had I known, I would have planned it differently.

5

The deadline for registration was approaching. Three investigators from the district office arrived at the Sanitation Department. The conductor carried an interesting document in his vest pocket — his parents' baptismal certificates. Dr. Pappenheim was taken aback, and he said: "I would not have believed it." Strange, the conductor wasn't pleased.

"You're welcome to join the Jewish order, if you like. It's a fine old order," said Pappenheim.

"I don't believe in religion."

"You can be a Jew without religion, if you like."

"Who said so — the Sanitation Department?"

It poured that afternoon. They gathered in the lobby, and served hot wine as on autumn days. Dr. Pappenheim was deep in a chess game with Semitzki. Towards evening, Frau Zauberblit's daughter arrived. From her father, General Von Schmidt, she had inherited an erect carriage, blonde hair, pink cheeks, and a deep voice. She was a student at a lyceum for girls, far away from her mother.

General Von Schmidt is still remembered here. They came to Badenheim the first year of their marriage, but Von Schmidt had hated it there, and called it Pappenheim, after the impresario. As far as he was concerned, it was no fit place for healthy people — no horses, no tennis, no hunting — no beer! They stopped coming after that and were gradually forgotten. They had a daughter. Years went by, and Von Schmidt, who had started his career as a lieutenant, rose through the ranks. Soon after, they were divorced. After the divorce, Frau Zauberblit, tall, slender, and suffering, appeared in Badenheim. That was the end of the matter.

The daughter stated at once that she had brought a document, a statement surrendering the so-called "rights of the mother." Frau Zauberblit studied the document and asked: "Is this what *you* wish?" "What my father wishes, and what I wish," she said like someone who had learned a part. Frau Zauberblit signed. It was a hard and abrupt farewell. "Excuse me, I'm in a hurry," she said on her way out. The daughter's appearance shook the hotel. Frau Zauberblit sat mutely in the corner. A strange new pride seemed to show on her face.

Throughout the hotel, a secret was uniting the people. The conductor felt ill at ease for some reason, and sat down with the musicians. The twins were to perform that night. The proprietor of the hotel was arranging the small auditorium. They haven't been seen on the veranda for two days now. Cloistered. "What do they do up there?" someone asked, and the headwaiter confirmed the fact that they had eaten nothing for two days. The people were standing by the windows, with the fading light on their faces. Pappenheim whispered. "They're rehearsing, aren't they wonderful?"

The silence of a house of prayer filled the small auditorium that evening. The audience was early, and Pappenheim darted back and forth between the doors as if that would make the twins come down before it was time. They came down precisely at eight o'clock, and took their place by the table. Pappenheim retreated towards the door, like a guard.

For two hours, they talked about death. They spoke in a calm, modulated voice, as if they had returned from Hell

and were no longer afraid. At the end of the recital, they
stood up. The people bowed their heads and did not
applaud. Pappenheim moved forward and took off his hat.
He seemed about to fall on his knees.

6

Apple strudel was served in the afternoon. Frau Zauberblit
had on her straw bonnet. Semitzki wore shorts, and
Pappenheim stood at the door like an unemployed actor. It
seemed as if the old days were back.

At midnight, the child prodigy arrived. The watchman
refused to let him pass, because he was not on the lists. And
Dr. Pappenheim, who was amused, said: "But can't you see
that he's Jewish?" When she heard, Frau Zauberblit said:
"Everything is going according to plan. Isn't that wonderful?"

"You'll love him too," Pappenheim whispered.

"The impresario is a man of his word. By the way — in
what language will the young artist sing?"

"Why — Yiddish of course — he'll sing in Yiddish."

When Pappenheim presented him, they saw before them
neither a child nor a man. He blushed, his suit was too long.
"What's your name?" asked Frau Zauberblit drawing near.
"His name is Nahum Slotzker — and speak slowly,"
Pappenheim interrupted, "he doesn't understand German."
Now they saw wrinkles around the eyes, but the face was
the face of a child. The adults were confusing him.

"Where are you from — Lodz?" asked Semitzki in Polish.

The boy smiled and said: "From Kalashin."

It was a strange evening. Frau Zauberblit was like a
retired gym instructor. The conductor shuffled cards and

joked with the cook. The cook gave him freshly baked poppyseed cakes. She was of mixed parentage. Orphaned at an early age, she had been for several years the mistress of Graf Schutzheim, until his death.

"Do you think they'll let me come too?" she asked slyly.

"There's no question about it. Who will cook for us in the land of cold?"

"But I'm not wholly Jewish."

"Well I'm not wholly anything."

"But your parents were both Jews, weren't they?"

"Yes, my dear, Jews by birth, but they converted to Christianity."

Next day, the patroness of the twins arrived in town. Frau Milbaum was tall and elegant, and she had an aura of majesty. Dr. Pappenheim was extremely glad to see her. He was always glad to see people returning to Badenheim.

The secret surrounds them little by little, a dread born of other intimations. They tread lightly, and speak in whispers. The waiters served strawberries and cream. The frenzied shadow of summer is spread out on the broad veranda. The twins sat beside Frau Milbaum, flushed and silent. They look like children in a roomful of adults. Pappenheim has planned a full program, and there is a strange sense of anticipation in the air. The old people die between one interrogation and the next. The town swims in alcoholic fumes. Last night at the café, Herr Furst fell down and died. For years he had passed through the streets in his magnificent clothes. Next door at the lottery house, another man died by the roulette table. Sometimes it seems not to be the alcohol but a freshness not from the nearby forests.

And the interrogations proceed quietly at the Sanitation Department. This is the center, and all the strands radiate from it. The Department is now omniscient. They have

maps, periodicals, a library — a person can sit and browse if
he wishes. The conductor registered at the Department and
came back smiling. They showed him a closetful of contracts,
licenses, and credentials. Strange — his father was the
author of an arithmetic book in Hebrew. "They know
everything, and they're happy to show a man his past," said
the conductor.

A barrier was erected at the town gate. No entrance, no
exit. But it was not a total blockade. The milkmen delivered
milk in the morning and the fruit truck unloaded its crates
at the hotel. Both cafés are open, and the band plays every
evening. Yet it seems that another time, from another place,
has broken through and is quietly entrenching itself.

7

The banquet given for the child prodigy began late. The
guests filed through the corridor, lamplight on their faces.
There were soft woolly shadows on the carpet. The waiters
served ice-cream in coffee. The tables were being laid in the
hall. A few musicians played to themselves in the corner.
Tongues of darkness climbed the long narrow windows.

Frau Milbaum sat on her throne, and green lights flashed
from her green eyes. People avoided her look. "Where are
my twins?" she asked in an undertone. No one answered.
They seemed caught in a net. The twins were talking to
Sally. Sally, in a long, flowered dress, was making faces like
a concert singer. The twins, who seldom conversed with
women, were embarrassed, and started to laugh.

Sally told them about the first festivals. Gerti appeared
and said, "You're here." "Please meet two real gentlemen,"
said Sally. The twins offered their long white hands. The

yanuka sat mutely in the corner. Dr. Pappenheim explained in broken Yiddish that the banquet was about to begin. Everyone was anxious to hear him sing.

The guests drank heavily. Frau Milbaum sat enthroned, and now there was venom in her green eyes. So here, too, her life was becoming involved. She thought that there was a plot against her. That morning she had registered at the Sanitation Department. The clerk did not take her titles into account, the ones bequeathed her by her first husband; and he did not so much as mention her second husband, a nobleman of the royal family. There was nothing on the form but her father's name.

Semitzki was chattering away gaily in faulty Polish. He turned good-naturedly to Frau Milbaum, and said: "Come and join our jolly circle. You'll find it amusing, I believe." Her look was metallic. "I am obliged," she said.

"A fine society — Jewish nobility," Semitzki was relentless.

"I understand," she said without looking.

"We would be delighted to have the lady's company," Semitzki continued to pique her.

"Don't worry, the Duchess will get used to us," whispered Zimbelmann the musician.

"She registered, didn't she? What's all this distance about?" added someone from the corner.

Frau Milbaum scanned them with her green eyes. "Riff-raff," she finally spat out the word.

"She calls us riff-raff," said Zimbelmann, "riff-raff she calls us."

The waiters served cheese wedges and Bordeaux wine. Dr. Pappenheim sat with the child prodigy. "There's nothing to fear. These are all very nice people. You'll stand on the stage and sing," he said, trying to encourage the boy.

"I'm afraid."

"Don't be afraid. They're very nice people."

The conductor emptied one glass after another. His face was turning red. "We're going to your native land, Semitzki. We must learn to drink."

"They drink real alcohol there — not beer soup."

"What will they do with a goy like me?"

"Don't worry, they'll only circumcise you," said Zimbelmann, but felt he had gone too far. "Don't worry. The Jews aren't babarians for all that."

Dr. Langmann approached the duchess and said: "I'm getting out of here tomorrow."

"But aren't you registered at the Sanitation Department?"

"I still consider myself a free citizen of Austria. They have to send the Polish Jews to Poland. That's the country for them. I'm here by mistake. One is entitled to a mistake, now and then, isn't one? You're also here by mistake. Are we to forfeit our freedom on account of a mistake?"

Now she scrutinized Sally and Gerti as they led the twins into a corner. "Whores," she glowered at them. The twins were greatly amused and as gay as two boys stumbling upon a wild party.

After midnight, they set the boy on the stage. He trembled. Dr. Pappenheim stood over him like a father. The boy sang about the dark forest, the haunt of the wolf. It was a kind of lullaby. Seated around the stage, the musicians stared dumbly. The world was collapsing before their very eyes. Someone said, "How wonderful!" Semitzki sobbed drunkenly. Frau Zauberblit approached him and asked: "What happened?"

At that moment, Sally felt an oppressive fear. "Dr. Pappenheim, may we go as well? Is there room for us?"

"What a question," he scowled at her, "There is room in our kingdom for every Jew and for everyone who wants to be a Jew. It is a mighty kingdom."

"I'm afraid."

"No need to fear, my dear, we'll all be going soon."

Gerti stood aside as though she had no right to ask questions.

8

The town is empty. The light no longer flowed. It seemed to have frozen, listening intently. An alien orange shadow nibbled stealthily at the geranium leaves. Bitter damp seeped into the thatch of the creeping vines. Pappenheim worries about the musicians. He treats them to chocolate, cream cake. Such kindness makes them submissive. No more quarrels. Now the light filters through the thick drapery and illuminates the wide veranda. Dr. Schutz's love is not so easy as in days gone by. The orange shadow lingers upon him and his beloved. The high-school girl burrows ever more deeply into his summer coat, as though afraid of a sudden parting.

The post office is shut down. A cold light falls on the smooth marble stairs. The gate with its Gothic relief conjures up a memorial in ruins. The night before, Pappenheim stood outside the post office and laughed, "Everything is closed."

As Pappenheim stood laughing on the stairs of the post office, a terrible struggle was in progress at the pharmacy. Two men from out of town grabbed the poison chest. Martin fought them, snatched the jars from their hands, and shouted after them, "I will not permit this." These two skeletal men had arrived a few days before. Their faces were cold with desperation.

Mandelbaum and his trio arrived like thieves in the night. Pappenheim took them downstairs, and brought tea.

"What happened?"

"We got a transfer," said Mandelbaum.

"Did you ask for it?"

"Of course we asked for it. A young man, a junior officer, has already sent on the documents. We told him that we had to get to the festival. He laughed, and he gave us a transfer. What do you say? We're in for it."

"That's wonderful," said Pappenheim. "Oh, I can't believe it. You need to rest."

"No, dear friend. That's not why we're here. We didn't have a chance to prepare anything. We have to rehearse."

The tin sun was fixed on the cold horizon. "How far is it from here to Vienna?" asked someone adrift in his own limp thoughts. "I'd say — two hundred kilometers, no more." These words hung in the air like tired ravens. The old favorite, apple strudel, was baking down in the kitchen. The sweet smell wafted on to the veranda.

"Why don't we ask for a visa?" said a musician who had traveled in his youth.

"Say you had a visa — where would you go?" The man was struck dumb by the question. The conductor put his card down and said: "As for me, I'm willing to go anywhere."

Martin took the winter clothes out of storage, and the house smelled of naphthaline. The dream of Poland calmed Trudy. Martin sits down and assures her, "In Poland, everything will be right. That's where we came from, and that's where we're bound. Those who were there have got to go back." There's music in his voice — Trudy listens and doesn't ask questions.

A group of angry people stood by the dead phone cursing the bureaucracy that, suddenly and without warning, had cut them off from their loved ones. Order, they grumbled, order. An energetic few wrote long letters of complaint. They described all the hardships that came from being disconnected. They claimed compensation from their travel agents, from all the authorities responsible for their being here. Of course, this was all futile. All telephone lines were disconnected, the post office was shut down. Domestic servants fled as if from a fire. The town began to live in a state of siege.

"What will they do to us in Poland?" asked one of the musicians.

"What do you mean? You'll be a musician as you've always been," answered a friend who dozed nearby.

"Then why all this moving around?"

"The force of circumstance," was the reply.

"Kill me, I don't understand. My common sense doesn't grasp it."

"In that case, kill your common sense and you'll start to understand."

Silence enveloped the houses. The withered vines grew wild. The acacia flourished. It was autumn and spring in a strange coupling. At night there is no air to breathe. Semitizki is on the bottle. He drinks like a peasant, mixes Polish and Yiddish. Of all his languages, the language of his childhood seems to be the only one left.

"Why are you drinking so much, dear?" asks Frau Zauberblit tenderly.

"When a man goes home he ought to be happy."

"It's cold there, really cold."

"Yes, but it's a pure, healthy cold, a cold with hope."

The registrations were over. The clerks at the Sanitation Department sit around, drinking tea. They've done their duty. Now they await orders.

But surprises never cease in the streets. Several days ago, a resident of Badenheim, who had been a major in the Great War, stood near the post office, and demanded to know why it was closed. Pappenheim, who had not given up his habit of a daily visit to the closed post office, answered, perhaps incautiously, that the town was cut off.

"I don't understand," said the major, "Is there a plague?"

"A Jewish plague."

"Are you trying to make fun of me?"

"No, I'm not. Try leaving." Turning his head with the narrow, metallic gaze that was used in scanning maps and fields, the major now focused on the short figure of Dr. Pappenheim, and seemed about to reprimand him and send him away.

"Haven't you registered at the Sanitation Department?" Pappenheim continued to harass him.

For two days, he fought the Department. He cursed the Jews and he cursed the bureaucracy. He terrorized the deserted streets of town. Finally, he shot himself in the head. Dr. Langmann, who never left the window, said to himself: you must admit, the Jews are an ugly people. I find them useless.

Just then, the conductor put down his cards and asked: "Do you remember anything from home?"

"Which home?" asked Blumenthal the musician, a simple man whose early life was a prolonged yawn. The conductor used to taunt him in the early days, but it was no use, he was wrapped up in his doze.

"From your Jewish home."

"Nothing."

"My parents converted, damn it."

"Then forget everything and go back to Vienna."

"My friend, I am in good standing at the Sanitation Department."

"What do they want of us?"

"It's hard to say," said the conductor as though faced with a difficult musical score. "If there's truth in those rumors that we're going to Poland, then we'd better start learning. I don't know a thing."

"At our age, we're a little rusty in the head, wouldn't you say?"

"There's no choice. We'll have to learn Polish."

"Is that how you imagine it?"

9

Gray days stretched across the town. Meals were no longer being served at the hotel. People queued by the serving hatch for dinner, barley soup and dry bread. The musicians opened their bags. A whiff of dead leaves and of drafty roads blew down the long corridors.

Suddenly, the old rabbi appeared in the street. Many years ago they'd brought him to Badenheim from the east. He had served as rabbi of the local synagogue, which was in fact an old-age home, until the last members had died, leaving the place empty. The rabbi had been stricken with paralysis. It was generally believed that he passed away with the others.

The proprietor of the hotel stood at the entrance and said, "Won't you come in, Sir?" — more like a doorman

than the proprietor of a hotel. Two musicians lifted the
wheel-chair. The rabbi shaded his eyes, and a blue vein
throbbed on his white forehead.

"Jews?" asked the rabbi.

"Jews," said the proprietor.

"And who is your rabbi?"

"You are. You are our rabbi."

The rabbi's face expressed some astonishment. His feeble
memory tried to discover if they were playing with him.

"Perhaps you will allow us to serve you a drink?"

The rabbi frowned: "Kosher?"

The proprietor lowered his eyes and did not answer.

"Everyone here is Jewish?" the rabbi recovered. There
was a sudden gleam of cunning in his eyes.

"Everyone, I believe."

"And what do you do?"

"Nothing," said the proprietor of the hotel, and smiled.
Semitzki rushed to his aid, "We're planning to go back to
Poland."

"What?" said the rabbi, straining to hear.

"To go back to Poland," repeated Semitzki.

The riddle was partially solved the next day. A kindly
Christian woman had nursed him all these years, then a few
days before she suddenly abandoned the house. After days
of trying to manipulate the wheel chair, the rabbi had
finally succeeded.

The rabbi poses questions, and the people answer him.
Many years of isolation made him forget the language, and
he speaks Yiddish sprinkled with the Holy Tongue. Some
musicians appeared in the doorway carrying luggage. "Who
are they?" asked the rabbi.

"Musicians."

"Are they going to play?"

"No, they want to go home, but the roads are barricaded."

"Let them spend the Sabbath with us."

"What did he say?" asked the astonished musicians.

The autumnal light, the tin light governs the town these days. The proprietor stands in the kitchen like one of the servants and ladles out soup. Supplies are not delivered. Provisions are running low. The dining room is like a soup-kitchen. Long shadows crawl on the tables at night. There is a faltering look in the eyes of the musicians. A few days ago they were still grumbling Now, their hopes are dashed. They comprehend: there is no going back. Pappenheim's optimism has also dissolved, the owner of the pastry shop shakes a fist at the hotel, or, more accurately, at Pappenheim, whom he threatens to murder.

"What does the rabbi say?" asked Frau Zauberblit.

"He's sleeping," whispered the proprietor.

The musicians took no pity on the hotel and stuffed their bags with crockery and silverware. Semitzki took them to task: "What for? No one uses fancy dishes in Poland." "What harm are we doing?" said one of them like an amateur thief. "If we come back, we'll return it."

The fleshy vines steal inside now, and spread over the veranda. This is their last burst of growth before winter. The forsaken chairs stand oafishly in place. A thick shadow nests inside the geranium pot. The flowers redden like rotten beets.

"What ever happened to the major?" asked someone.

"He killed himself."

By the shuttered windows of the pastry shop stands Bertha Stummglanz. They brought her here last night. Her parents died some years before, and the house was transferred to the local council.

"Do you remember me?" asked Sally.

"I think I do, I think we were schoolmates."

"No, dear. My name is Sally and this is Gerti."

"Oh, I've made a mistake then, haven't I?" said Bertha apologetically.

"My name is Sally and this is Gerti."

Bertha could not remember. Her memory was evidently deserting her. Her eyes wandered aimlessly.

"Why is everything closed?"

"The town is being transferred. Dr. Pappenheim says that everything is going to Poland, including us."

"Dr. Pappenheim?"

"The impresario, don't you remember him?"

Strangers are brought in from the gate. Dr. Pappenheim stands at the entrance of the hotel like a doorman.

"Why did you come here?" someone asked.

"They were born here, so they had to come back."

"It's a fine place," Dr. Pappenheim interjects. "Mandelbaum is with us, the twins are with us."

"The twins? Who are the twins?"

"Where are you from, Jews?" asked the rabbi. An ancient grief glazed his eyes.

"This is our rabbi," says Pappenheim proudly, "A real one of the old school."

The rabbi's questions never stop. The proprietor wears a skull-cap, and serves him cold water.

No end to surprises. Last night, Helena came home. Her husband the lieutenant threw her off the estate. She has the face of her ailing mother. Incredulous, Trudy stroked her hands like a blind woman. Martin was drunk with joy. "Now we can go. Together we can go anywhere."

Every day brings more newcomers, descendants of former Badenheimers. The town's curse had pursued them all these years, and now they were caught. Dr. Pappenheim received a letter from the Sanitation Department, instructing him to put his articles at its disposal. Pappenheim rejected — a grand tour awaits us!

Autumn turned to dust. The wind growled in the empty streets. Mandelbaum tortures the trio, polishes the music. The twins are cloistered again. An air of gravity pervades the hotel. Pappenheim walks on tiptoe, saying, "Hush, hush, you're disturbing the sound." The musicians quietly nibble their bread. "Practice won't do us any good. It's too late now for what you didn't accomplish when you were young." Pappenheim comforts them: "In the new place, there'll be time, you'll be able to practise. Where there's a will there's a way." He himself plans to take up research.

Dr. Pappenheim makes continuing efforts to talk to the owner of the pastry shop. "Why be angry with us? What have we done: we haven't committed a crime, after all. Tell us what our crime is. In Poland, you can open up a bigger shop. A person has to broaden his horizons." Wasted words. The owner of the shop stands at the window, raving: "If it weren't for this hotel, if it weren't for the corruption, they wouldn't have closed the town. It's all because of Pappenheim. He ought to be arrested." He only stops at night.

Mandelbaum looks happier. The trio is inspiring him. He is getting new tones from his violin.

"When do we set off?" he asks Pappenheim, the way he used to ask his agent.

"Soon," says Pappenheim like the bearer of a secret.

"We're improving, we're improving."

It poured on Saturday night. The rabbi prayed loudly. People hugged the walls like shadows. The proprietor brought wine and candles, and the rabbi performed the Havdalah service.

Immediately after the Havdalah, the musicians went off

to pack. The bags were big and swollen. Dr. Pappenheim was surprised at the commotion, and said, "I'm going like this — empty-handed. If they want me, they'll take me like this — empty-handed."

The next day was bright and cold. Mandelbaum rose early and stood with the trio on the smooth steps of the hotel. The rehearsals had left their mark. His distinguished brow had turned white. Semitzki escorted Frau Zauberblit with a cumbersome elegance. Professor Fusshalt stood in his bathrobe as if he'd been shaken out of a fitful sleep: "The proofs, what will happen to the proofs?" Zimbelmann the musician wrapped the rabbi in two velvet blankets and put him in his wheel-chair. The proprietor said: "What must we bring?" "Nothing, don't worry," said Pappenheim. By the old ornamented gate, the clerk called the roll. The people answered their names as at a morning parade. A long journey stretched before them. At the familiar railway station there stood a hissing engine with many empty carriages. No one pushed. No one cried.

Translated by Betsy Rosenberg

A Village Death

YITZHAK BEN NER

1

The day before yesterday, after the rain, was perhaps the last time that my wife, Yota, would raise her head and gaze out of her bedroom window at the stretch of alien land on which she had been passing her days in grief. Under leaden skies, she waited for the grave.

During the rainy season, all seven roads leading to the village-circle glistened with the water that fills the wheel ruts. Even those roads that wagons haven't crossed for years. Under dark skies, the village-circle glistens hopelessly, a sun with seven rays like those drawings we used to make when we were kids. My wife's lips moved as she looked out the window. Maybe she was silently cursing my village and its inhabitants. I really don't know.

A week ago, along the road that passes near her window, sixteen-year-old Robbie Tzuri, driving his father's tractor, had flattened a three-year-old child from the city who was staying with one of our neighbors. The child was immediately taken to a hospital in Haifa, his back crushed, and the police took Robbie in for investigation. When I returned from the cemetery where I worked, I watched how they put the boy, who looked thunderstruck, into their

patrol car. During the following days, the village council did
everything to calm things down and to straighten out the
tragic affair. Robbi hadn't had a driver's license and things
were really complicated. But, if I'm not mistaken, in the
end, they succeeded in getting him off. Whether for better
or worse, the council always tries to keep such incidents
within the confines of the village.

I was born in this village and I love it dearly. It and its
people; its fields and gardens; its winter and summer skies;
the cobbled roads; its granaries, chicken coops, barns, and
lawns; the roar of its tractors and the circle of its tall, thick
cypresses that stand sharpened against the sky and whose
needles are like green fur, dark, softly shadowed and hiding
secrets. I love its children, its roads — dirt roads — dusty in
the summertime and muddy in the winter; the straw that
drifts in the wind; its streets, the many cows that gaze with
astonishment through their glazed and liquid eyes beyond
the iron fences; the cackling of chickens, the ordinary
conversations between friends who happened to meet; the
sucking sound of the pipe that draws milk from the cans,
and the smell of fresh bread which is still baked in squares
and is coarse; the sunburnt boys and the narrowly built girls
who though pretty are also a bit vulgar. I like the contours
of the stone highway that runs around my village and the
narrow road that is swallowed by the darkness of the orange
groves; the clicking of the water sprinkler hammerheads and
the sprays; the chirping of the birds that gup the tree
branches; the trees; the clouds of flour dust that settle upon
the silos; the children who trample with their boots in the
mud puddles near the garage; the pigeons resting on the tall
eucalyptus trees; the abandoned railroad tracks overgrown
with grass; and the fields of fodder, the clover, the sorghum,
the barley, the cotton and corn. I love the hot, dead hours

in the summer glare, the horizon beyond the hills whose last longing rays cut across my village.

My love for this village is great. I love it for its industriousness, its gardens, grass, livestock, its accomplishments, even if that love is not reciprocated. For who am I? I'm ready to give my life for this village and its people. They are the hope of everything that will and might be accomplished. There are times when I want to stand up and call out to the whole community: rise up, my beloved ones and prepare to defend yourselves. The world is about to explode. Sword clashes with sword and fire consumes fire. A terrible and huge abyss gapes open to swallow all; the evil and those less so. This village of mine is an island of beauty and purity tucked away in a corner of the earth. Its people are diligent, without cunning, and never harm one another. They do their work, and a green peacefulness, of labor properly done hovers over all. The mounds of eggs grow taller and taller; milk flows in clear streams; oranges golden as far as the eye can see. And it's good.

I keep asking myself: how will this good be preserved? And in despair I try to shelter this green, tranquil island of hard work, honesty and quiet love and understanding and companionship, a love which doesn't burst forth in tedious words such as mine. How shall I shelter it from the frauds of the world beyond its sphere; from the insidious intrigues, from incipient evil, from unruliness, discontentment so irritating and perverting? I see our sons returning from the army and the serenity that once veiled their eyes slowly turns into apprehension, disquiet, causing a tremor of confusion and uncertainty. Because the world is storming the narrow barriers erected by the village life, they are no longer the same boys. They mature too quickly and are no longer sure of what once was or what will be. The alien world planted doubt, dread, dissatisfaction in them.

I'm a tall man and when I stand erect people say, that whether I like it or not, I put the fear of God in strangers. I'm a powerful man. I was sixteen years old when soldiers from Jordan's Arab Legion wandered into my father's vineyard to pick some grapes. I stood there, one against three and beat the hell out of them. One of them had aimed a British rifle at me and I broke it over my knee. Their corporal, who was at least as husky as I was, had to be hospitalized later in Haifa. For two days I hid from the police among the bushes lining the old cemetery. Only then did Natan Gordon, one of the village councilmen, convince me to turn myself in. For three weeks I sat in the Lower Haifa jail together with three brothers, thieves from Tyre, and a cheating peddler from Yokneam, while my village strove day and night, pleading on my behalf until they got me released without even a trial. For this and for other things they have done for me throughout my life, I'm grateful. It's why I want to stand at our village entrance, spread my arms over all whom I love and defend them. Let all its men and women, children and infants come and find shelter in my shadow so that they will never be troubled, and the green, refreshing tranquility will flood over them for the rest of their lives.

I'm forty-three years old today and what hair I have left is all gray. All the hair of my arms and chest is gray. But because I was first to be born among the settlers on this hill, I'm still counted among its young. Many who are younger than I am, are parents to maturing boys and girls and they too are considered young. I myself faithfully continue to attend the youth gatherings and parties. Never would my wife, Yota, condescend to join me. I sit with the others though I'm alone and make every effort to partake in what goes on, always trying not to embarrass others. For I know that I don't really belong among these young people who casually sprawl upon the cement floor and crack seeds; nor do I belong among the young girls in short dresses and rosy cheeks. There's a wide age gap between us. When my mother became pregnant with my twin brother and me, the founders of our village were furious. In those days everyone lived in one tin shack, one couple to a compartment, and they had all decided that they wouldn't have children until they could afford to build individual huts. Bad luck held up the Jewish Agency's building project, and then an epidemic broke out in the village so that again childbearing had to be postponed. And so I'm three years older than the first children who followed me. Look at me and look at them: thin, quiet, charming, their hair still black, their teeth still glistening when they smile, and they remain young. Life is theirs. As the days go by I grow more distance from them. I'm a stranger among them.

Was I ever like them? I used to play on an abandoned mound of earth alone in the shade of a pine tree. My twin brother died soon after he was born and at times my mother would talk about him when she was still alive. He had blond hair and dark eyes, she used to say movingly. Well, my father would always say consolingly, you know that the color of infants' eyes and hair changes when they grow up. No, no, my mother would retort, as if in my brother's case it was some miracle. Alone on the abandoned mound of earth, in the shade of the pines, a small girl, almost a baby, in a very thin, stained dress, had been looking at me from a distance and didn't dare come close. Maybe I sucked strength and vitality from my brother and he died because of me, I used to think sullenly, pulverizing the dirt while the girl had looked on. Maybe I was already grown up by then and was big enough to frighten her.

These days, as I watch over my wife, Yota, as she dies, I glance at a few photographs of my childhood and I observe myself: hair clipped, narrow forehead, looking straight ahead; I'm still a kid but already my eyebrows are thick, my mouth is pursed, my shoulders hunched; I wear three quarter length pants and heavy shoes without socks. The photo reveals a distance which acts as a barrier between me and the other children of the second grade of the neighboring village school which we attended. They are my age: arms thrown about each other's shoulders, playful to the point that their exuberance shouts out of the old photograph. And I stand aside, scowling, rigid, strange; waiting for the photographer to snap his shot and let me be. I'm still that way. Not old yet and I'm already graying, and at times feeling a thin veil of fog over my eyes. I see everything from a distance, detached. The inhabitants of my village are active people. The tractors come and go, the wagons laden with crops; children joyously shouting between the water sprinklers in the swimming pool, and the sunburnt women gossip loudly amongst themselves as they move along the shelves of the grocery store. The village loves its life, is rejuvenated by it, while in me there is no youth left. Almost.

My wife, Yota, who is six years older than I am, is also an old woman, actually on her death-bed. She's only forty-nine and her cramped life, which had by then been shaken twice and destroyed once, is already behind her. A few years after we were married, her body began to disintegrate and she became slovenly. Before she took to her bed, when she still walked about and did some housework, her dressing gown was wrinkled and torn, her hair already fading and gathered in an unkempt bun. Even then her eyes were red, and at night she'd wait until I closed mine before she would begin to cry. Many a night she'd cry to herself, and I would

become angry with myself thinking about it, alone, in my
solitary work during the day. It was then that I wanted her
to like what I liked in this parcel of green land and in these
people among whom we lived. But she couldn't care less.
Quietly, stubbornly, in a fury, she refused to love what I
loved. I don't blame her now. It's many a year since we
found something to say to each other. The passionate days
are gone, and not even a tremor of joy goes through me
when I recall those nights and days, naked, on sheets
drenched with sweat, between uncovered, trembling white
thighs anticipating pleasure, arms outstretched, grasping and
entwined, mouths desiring and never satisfied, panting,
groaning so that the whole blissful moment makes the flesh
quiver. As if she was not the woman of then. Come to me.
Stolen from her husband. Cut off from memories and love
and from partnership and endless patience; from a home
whose life was ordered. In my room, in the old shack in my
parents' yard, behind the shuttered windows and the closed
door, between tar-papered walls and under the scorching tin
roof, we're torn and being torn. A young woman,
pale-skinned, full-bodied, lovely and provoking, who blushes
as if I'm her first lover. And her blue eyes and her
astonished mouth seem incapable of hiding the intensity of
her desire. Her hair is bright yellow, her hips are wide, and
her breasts heavy and soft. She's a Gentile whose husband
had brought her from Poland. They knew he was Jewish,
but no one knew for sure if she had ever converted.
However, since they lived together in our village, no one
gave the problem a second thought. No one. Not even the
rabbi, who later married us, caused any difficulties, nor did
he investigate the matter by making inquiries at the
Rabbinate. Only the old parents of the villagers used to turn
their heads when she would pass by, as if she were a whore.

Now it's years since she walked down the village street and it's I who take care of all the shopping. When she dies, will they investigate about her religion? Suddenly I dread the fact as I sit in the adjoining room and wait. In the course of the twenty-two years of our life together, I never once asked her if she had converted and I never sought to discover if she secretly kept some vestiges of the faith she was raised in. In those hours of love making, without reckoning, timeless, without fear, with all the guilts, the ache, sorrow, the lust, the hate, when the pleasure would make her mindless, she would, in a choked voice, let slip the name of Jesus, and her whole body that clung to me would shudder from an intense and joyous pain, as though at that moment the finger of God had touched her.

And the sweat used to pour off us and soak into the sheets, oozing more and more from our skins, and the tin roof burned from the sun. My father, my dead father, probably must have sighed in the shade of his vineyard. He knew everything but said nothing. How I embittered his life, and yet he never reprimanded me. She and I would be glued to each other in the open, consumed by the burning sun which ignited the seven roads leading to my village. And Yota, my beloved, whom I had abducted, screeches through lips bitten till they bleed; Jesus! Jesus! But now when I conjure up those memories, they do not arouse any yearning or beauty. Nothing.

2

I understand now what a horrible thing I had done many years ago. It was terrible injustice. And all of us who were touched by it are constantly within arm's reach of each other, on the same small parcel of land, and unable to break away and escape. Every day I see her son, Uri, and her daughter, Iza. They're grown up now and have their own families and farms, and on the face of it, all seems to have turned out well. I even see her husband, Beno. In my own mind, I still address him as *her husband,* and at times, in the few words I used to exchange with her, I'd say, *your husband* right to her ears even though she's divorced from him and has been my lawful wedded wife for twenty-one years. We did a terrible thing to them as well as to ourselves, but it isn't only because of this that Yota and I grew apart and that it's at least ten years since we've had any need for each other. On the contrary, all her reflections are in the past: about her husband, Beno, her son Uri and her daughter, Iza. They're her whole life now and I have no part in all this but for a few memories that are hidden within her — shaming her perhaps from time to time when they seethe in her fever-tormented brain — and in the few routine concerns that still interest her before she took to her bed never to rise again. As for myself I'm ready to love her as before. I could still find some love in me, some devotion to her, if I really tried. But since she's shown no interest, I let it pass.

We remain silent and in never ending pain we repent for our misdeeds, for our evil hearts, for this horrible act which we perpetrated. And this unfortunate woman, who shares with me this half empty, gloomy house, with its cracked walls, is no less to blame than I am. For she did as she wished to do, this mother of two, more mature and experienced than myself, a woman who in her wanderings and tribulations started life anew, while I was only twenty years old when we met, a boy whose evil thoughts exceeded his experiences. Nevertheless long ago I was ready to take

full punishment, heavy as it might be, certainly greater than
the meager reward that was short and quick, like lightning.
I'm not afraid of anything. I walked into this by myself and
I have no hope for the future, one way or another. I'm not
the man who shall dwell in God's tent nor will I attend Him
on His holy mountain. The truth came too late to me, but
now that it's come, I'm ready for everything. Let me atone
for everything and expiate my village, its people; my wife,
who squandered away her life with me; her husband, Beno,
who always lowered his eyes when we happened to pass
each other on the village lanes, and their children who
occasionally knock on the door of my house and who when
I open up ask with embarrassment: "Is mother home?" as if
she ever left her house of suffering, and then they would
disappear into her room and to their secrets.

After years, some of the pain thawed — the blackness, the
guilts — and she consoled herself through her children. I
worked hard for that, though indirectly, through others,
practically pleading. Finally they came to her. First the
daughter, Iza, before she left for the army. Like a thief,
she'd come and go to her. After a while the son came as
well. He was older and had witnessed the beginning and he
remembered. He would come and visit my pining and
grieving wife, even brought his own wife and baby. Again I
saw an opaque light in Yota's eyes. There was no way back,
but suddenly distances were shortened. No longer light
years. Only a few paces. The years passed.

I was a young buck then. The village girls serving in the
army who laughed at my predicament merely increased my
desires. And when I returned from doing my own service,
and she, her husband, the boy and the infant girl moved
into the small shack opposite the deserted youth center that
stood amidst overgrown grass, things began to get

complicated. At the time her husband, Beno, was a village official. He was a short man, thin and neat, his hair combed flat, and whether it was summer or winter he always wore clothes made of wool. During the day, when he toiled over his paperwork, or at night, when he sat for a long time in his office, or when he did his army reserve duty, his wife clung to me. How did it all start? It just began. Almost without saying a word. As if by itself. I was helping them take apart the slats of a large wood crate in which they had brought most of their belongings from Europe. She gives me a drink. No. Just plain water from the ice box. I smash a large cake of ice for her and put a few chips on my sweating back. I catch her looking at me. She's laughing, and I take some ice chips and rub her face in them. She struggles with me, laughing, and her eyes hide nothing. I seduce her for the first time in the wild grass. The infant girl sleeps in the shack, her son's in the kindergarten and her husband's at his office. On the village road, a stone's throw away, wagons pass loaded with sacks of chicken feed, and women carry baskets to and from the grocery store. And we're stuck together like animals, and what's been pent up in me all the years is discharged into her. Endlessly. And there is no end to her desire for it all. No end to it at all.

In a few months — our place is relatively small, but I was shameless then — everything's out in the open. Everyone knows. People speak about it secretly and then openly. My father looks at me in a different way, worried. No one blames me. I don't blame anyone. Very likely the village council hesitates to interfere in people's personal affairs. I've always been a little strange to them, and in their eyes, she's a whorish *goyeh*. From all these things, from the smiles, the whispers, from the looks, her husband attempts suicide. His son, Uri, finds him with his wrists slashed in the

abandoned youth cehter, near his shack, on a stack of
newspapers that had been collected for the army and never
delivered, his glasses neatly tucked into the pocket of his
wool jacket, his tie tightly knotted and his mouth pressed
closed as if reconciled to this last torture. At that moment
I'm with his wife. His child finds us glued together, and like
a grown-up, he calls to me. Me. Yes, me.

I carry her husband, a sad bundle of bones, all the way to
the infirmary, and until we get there, the blood from his cut
wrists pours over me and on to the grass and on the village
streets. They revive him against his will, and all that night, I
sit in my old hideout in the cemetery so as not to face my
father. The next day I go down to the farm, and avoiding
my father's eyes, I ask him to sell the little fruit he has
grown in order to give me some money to ship out from the
port of Haifa.

At the time there was a seamen's strike there and the
shipping companies were looking for replacements. Without
concern for the strikers, I hired on. I was like an escaped
convict. I wanted to obliterate everything, to torment
myself by forgetting all that had happened. A man fleeing.
But when I arrived in Cyprus, I longed so for my father and
my village, the country, for that woman, Yota, for her
husband who survived to live with his shame, for the rutted
roads, for the vineyards. All kinds of dreams and forgetfulness sprouted within me and like a spoiled child, I debarked
at Famagusta. I had no money and a wire was sent from our
Consulate to my village council. The following day a wire
arrived guaranteeing a return ticket, and that same evening I
was on my way to Haifa on a boat carrying fruit from
Yugoslavia. One more day and I was in my village. Coming
up the side road like a thief, I entered my house and there
my father informed me that her husband was alive. Till this

day my father's eyes burn the back of my neck. Till this very day.

After that, maybe for half a year or more, Yota and I avoid meeting so that we don't lose control of ourselves. She locks herself into her shack, and when she does go out, everyone stares at her. She's a stranger here, so her humiliation is greater than mine. Every day her husband finishes his work at the same time, collects his son and daughter, and together with his wife, their adulterous mother, they lock themselves away in their shack. Once, I couldn't stand it any longer and I went out at night into the wild grass in which a boy can stand tall and unseen, I knelt there facing her window, which was lighted by a paraffin lamp, and I waited. All that night I waited in the grass. My clothes were soaked with dew, and the mad desire for her hot body burned inside me.

Throughout that night I couldn't forget her and she couldn't forget me, and the next day everything started again swirling back upon us. Her husband went to work, spotted me and then turned away as if he didn't see me. She came out and noticed me. Her face turned white and she froze. We faced each other in this way, and on the path beyond the grass, the whole village stared at us.

After that everything was in the open — almost — and her husband reconciled himself to the facts. She would spend whole nights with me in the shack in our yard and nothing mattered. I avoided my father's eyes and she saw her children only fleetingly, before their father came to take them back to school. The village avoided him. Me, having been born there and known to be strange, they forgave for better or for worse. Her, the outsider, they blamed for everything. Without words. Without saying a thing. And when after a long, painful illness my father died, God bless

him, and was buried in our cemetery alongside my mother,
our village council spent much time mediating until Beno,
her husband, agreed to a divorce. That was when they urged
us to get married as soon as possible.

Using chance witnesses off the street, we were married in
the courtyard of the Haifa Rabbinate. I wore a white shirt
and my father's striped pants which were refitted too
tightly, and she, the stranger in our midst, stood in a white
dress, a bouquet of roses in her hands. One of our village
councilmen was at my side. Yota had no one but me. As I
undress her in that rundown hotel on the Street of the
Prophets, my wife begins to cry bitterly, like a calf led to
slaughter. She cried through the night. She has never cried
before. She cries and I turn her over and make love to her
with a passion as great as my fury against her, against myself
and against her crying.

The people of my village are good people. They gave her
husband and his children a house to console them a little in
their humiliation and maybe also in order not to allow the
scandal outside the circle of these cypresses. They even
compensated him with a Yemenite maid who saw to the
household tasks, his meals, his clothes. In this way they
tried to make amends, little as it might seem to him, for
what I had destroyed. I and this woman. And for me they
did what they had done for Barukh Zerubavel, the crazy
one, who had slept with a girl from an immigrant transit
camp and made her pregnant, a fact which compelled them
to appease her parents and arrange the whole business of
getting rid of the infant. We couldn't stand the looks they
gave us, the silences and the fact that they all knew us, and
since the ambiance in the village became unpleasant, against
my will and for her sake, I accepted the advice of the
council and we moved away. We settled in Hedera and I

worked in the citrus packing house. The year we spent there
was horrible. I walked around suffocating. We didn't have
children and I don't even want to talk about that. I walked
around and I suffocated. I can't bear being outside my
village even if my life there turns to hell. I just can't. I yearn
for my village and she for her children. And by now
contrition begins to seethe in her and we find no solace in
each other. The little happiness we had is already over.
Finished.

And so I donned the same clothes I wore for my
marriage, took a day off and that morning came before the
village council and begged them to save me. I'm not a man
of many words, but at the time I found the words, and the
council reconciled themselves to taking us back. I'm one of
them and they are like me. After a year we returned to the
village, ready to take up any burden — looks, memories,
accusations, scorn, loneliness. I can't live outside my village.
I just can't.

With my father's old sickle, I cut the grasses that had
overgrown the garden around the old, abandoned house of
my parents. I chopped down the old, wood, tar-papered
shack, temple of our concupiscence, with his ax and sealed
its cracked walls with plaster. And here I am a homeowner
with a farm, a wife, all in my old native, lovely village. And
slowly, through its distractions, my village calmed my rage,
giving back to me a little of that peace of mind and a feeling
of fulfillment.

I'm thankful to my village and its people. A fine, invisible
thread ties us into one family, the good and the bad; the
saintly and the sinful; in purity and in beauty. I'm grateful
to them for forgiving me and for taking me back amongst
them. I love them all. I sit in the large moviehouse with its
tiled roof and through whose windows the wind bursts, and

I don't look at the screen because in the dim, flickering light, I'm examining the faces of my people. Young people and old ones; parents and parents of parents. A strong stock. Backs bent from toil. Blouses made of rough cloth. Creases across their napes. Hair growing unkempt out of their temples. Large, comforting hands. Calm gazes. Quiet curiosity, somewhat distant. Often I stop short along the village lanes in order to look at these people and try to absorb within me that which they possess but which I unfortunately cannot. The power of this place; the color of the silence; the beauty of the whole soul. I have faith in them. Only in them. Out of them comes hope for the world.

3

Since we've returned, I rarely leave my village. Dreams of the wide world don't plague me. I know. The world is marching toward its destruction. With a kind of sick hunger, I spend much time reading newspapers. I read every paper that falls into my hands from beginning to end. I read many books as well and quickly absorb them so that no fact is lost to me. I'm aware that in the eyes of the villagers this adds to my strangeness. I'm big, and bulky and without any presence. My clothes are wrinkled, skimpy and unbecoming; it's as if my strength bursts through them gracelessly. And yet I'm filled to the brim with the wisdom of the innumerable books that I've read. Never will I draw from the well of knowledge that's stored in this heavy, square head of mine. Yes, I have much trouble expressing myself when I chat with the villagers, and my words are curt and few. When someone approaches me casually, even with small talk, something pounds in my head and gives me no peace.

I'm overwrought by contact. At times, a neighbor asks that
I help him with the milking or hay-stacking, and I drop
whatever I'm doing and come immediately. I find it hard to
say things, but everyone knows that despite my peculi-
arities, I read and write three languages besides Hebrew
fluently; English, French and German, all learned on my
own. With the aid of dictionaries, I stacked volume upon
volume into a storehouse that refused to become full, and
the strange words which until this day I haven't had the
opportunity to pronounce have been fixed in my head.
They're conceived by me as letters, not sounds. I think that
in the eyes of the villagers I'm a man of contradictions and
they don't know whether to ridicule me or pay me respect,
since I've never found a way to draw upon my treasure. But
I didn't come to speak about myself, but rather about the
fears I have for my village and my compassion for its
inhabitants.

I have compassion for my village because it pains me to
see this bastion of solitude and truth within the world
disintegrate. I see the signs of the holocaust that threaten,
and the clues of madness that are encroaching upon us all:
to destroy, to devastate, and without mercy. Everyone is
going insane. I glance at the prophetic columns of the
weeklies. I hear the screaming announcements on the radio,
learn about the youth seeking new experiences through
drugs. I know of the renewed, strange yearnings for God,
and I wonder over the naiveté of all the idealists and the
peaceniks. I see the roads jammed with countless cars that
screech nervously as they fly by, and listen to the masses
who are looking for leaders to guide them and there's only
great confusion and fear and loss. They all have a part in
this madness. Everyone deceives everyone; everyone
suspects everyone; everyone torments everyone; everyone

degrades everyone. Hypocrites, devious intimidators. No
one doubts himself and things are polarized between good
and bad. Everyone inoculates himself against the misfortune
of another. Everyone. Myself included. How many times,
while I'm eating my breakfast and feeling sorry for myself,
do I hear the radio announce in a metallic voice that one
hundred and twenty people drowned in a typhoon on
Okinawa, or that a father slaughtered his three children in
Seattle, U.S.A., and my peace of mind is hardly disturbed?
How is it that the world isn't shaken over and over again?
How come I don't go out of my mind when I hear of such a
horror, such a tragedy, death? One hundred and twenty all
at once. Three children murdered; a children's bus that hit a
mine, and I sit and chew bread baked in this village and
drink milk from its dairy, and but for my brain which
chastises my heart, I feel nothing.

Later on, I think it over and understand that it's better
this way. Much better. We have to shelter ourselves, to
harden our feelings, because if we don't, we'll go crazy from
all the horror of the world. Yes, I think to myself, we have
to raise a thick wall within us and let all the bad smash itself
against it. Until here and no further. No one is capable of
absorbing the pain and sickness of his generation because
one would go mad from the different kinds of death, the
violence; from the deviousness, the poverty, the hunger;
from the misfortune; from the hypocrisy; from the tensions,
the despair; from narrow-mindedness; from stupidity; from
ugliness — and especially the fear. For we all fear what
awaits us beyond this fog. This fear pursues me relentlessly.

Mind you, I'm not concerned about myself. Not even for
my wife, Yota. We, ours, is over and done with, and I accept
the end. Until this day I fear the idea that someone dear to
me in my village will come and stand on the road that leads

down to the highway and raise his eyes to the world and see the catastrophe that swirls like a whirlpool ready to engulf all and to suck everything into it, to wreck everything, to turn everything into a cloud of chaff, and then, having no protection, all this green will be destroyed, all the lovely, precious tranquillity that's stored here on this little, out-of-the-way hill destroyed forever. Fear of this encroaching catastrophe grips me each time I think about it and again I try to explain that it's not because of me but because of the place and its destiny, because of its people and their purpose. I try to prevent them from opening their eyes. The longer they fail to see the evil storm that's brewing and about to eradicate them from this sinful world, the better. That's why I try at times, to go out to the crossroads at the village gate and stand there ahead of them all, spreading my arms and not allowing anything to happen. I'm very capable of defending my village and its inhabitants.

That's why I wish to keep pain and agony from those I love, so that they'll never know anguish. Many of the grand-parents — white-bearded and wrinkled — have died. The parents themselves are grandparents and aged. Every now and then one of the village founders passes away and his death carries with it a hidden fear in the hearts of those who remain alive. The beautiful synagogue, that was built in its time for the old folks, is practically empty. I've begun to visit there wearing my work hat, and I try to ease a bit the loneliness of the few remaining old people who keep vigil over the building. They nod to me in welcome or maybe in wonder, their lips mumbling prayers. I bend over the thick, holy tomes and try to comfort my weary brain as I search for wisdom and nonsense between the lines, and from the large windows facing westward, I see the sunset that threatens to cover the village in red. A wind from the mountains cools my burning brow, and my mouth, as if of itself, whispers the evening prayer, and even though I don't want to be heard, my whisper bursts forth like thunder.

I continue to go to the synagogue and I'm almost a regular member. On the Sabbath and on holidays, we are many, most of whom are not truly believers and don't follow all the laws. Whether from fear of life's end or of the mystery of what's beyond it, we come to pray and are united in our efforts to keep off the Day of Judgment. During the weekdays we're about fifteen people in this large village founded forty-five years ago and whose inhabitants number nine hundred and seventy-three. Days pass and one of our places becomes empty and we follow the man to his rest. I then read in the eyes of my fellow villagers the pain of death. Only my wife, Yota, whose eyes sparkle dully with bitter joy, which is both tortured and mocking, says nothing when I tell her about the death of one villager or another.

The news of death is terrible. One day, nearly seven years ago, an army jeep stopped before the Brock house and the officer notified them that their son Elad was shot dead. Until this day I remember his mother's scream. She's a good woman, quiet, diligent. Because her husband has a heart condition, the burden of running the farm is on her and she's always harassed with work. She never raised her voice till then. Until this day her scream tears through me, piercing and long. Not human. From a strange world. Endless. In one breath.

Another time a grown calf with sharp horns gored Ephraim Shekhner in the gut. He was bedridden for three months, suffering all the time before he finally died, his screams rising and slashing across the solitude of the village. No medication nor drug could calm him.

And now Margolit, eighty-seven years old, suddenly sunk on his cane on the village road — all of him, with his lean, straight back and his silken, white beard, the pride and beauty of age. His son Ze'ev Margolit, fifty-five years old or more, father to grown children, falls on the body, shocked, and cries like a baby: "Aba! Aba!" and tries vainly to open his father's eyes out of which the spark was extinguished all at once.

Now Zafrira Katzov had hugged the tombstone of her husband — by then buried three years, killed in the war — when everyone went up to the cemetery to bury Pinhas Horowitz. Her love was so strong and undying that she broke away from the others and knelt by her husband's grave, unable to tear herself away, while her wails grew louder and louder. When they pulled her away, my heart was torn by her screeching.

My life doesn't matter and I don't look for much pleasure in this world. What little peace I have at times, which cools my feverish and constantly thinking brain, I find in reading. I'm still incapable of weaning myself from physical desire, and since my wife and I have long ago ceased making love, I slip away furtively when I'm aroused and go to those coarse whores at the Stanton in Haifa. Once a month, maybe twice. Like a thief. I'm ashamed of this. The young men of our village never had to spend their energies on the likes of these, but still I have such needs from time to time, and I only hope that none of the villagers ever finds out. Those girls think I'm a widower from one of the kibbutzim. I never let on more than that. I don't go to them for conversation.

These are the only pleasures that I seek for myself nowadays. No more. I'm ready to give all to my village. I'm prepared to gather all the grief of those villagers I love, and it matters little to me if they don't realize how much I love them. Four years ago I sold my cows and went to the town hall to ask the council to assign me the job of caring for the dying and the dead. They were amazed, but long ago they had come to realize how strange I was and they reconciled themselves to my proposal. And so more and more I spend my time giving succor to others' grief. I'm the man who's informed of every death. A woman dies in childbirth, a boy from the village is shot dead on guard duty, a father passes away, or one of us is killed in a road accident — this is a large village and we have ten to a dozen deaths a year — and they hurry to let me know, and I go willingly, filled with compassion and with all my strength to inform the bereaved. I don't know how to soften the blow and I really don't try to. I absorb the confusion, the shock and the first burst of pain. I look directly at the bereaved, I grab them when they collapse. And at times, unconsciously, they bury their heads against my chest and cry quietly or aloud, and an endless tremor of love and sadness passes from them to me. Sometimes they push me away in silence and try to steady themselves. I see the blank terror in their eyes that look back into mine, the strange trembling that grips them, and their soundless, gaping mouths.

I see all this and I try to distract them from death, since they will live on. But I really don't know how. If only people would accept death as a natural phenomenon, reconcile themselves fully to it without so much pain, it would be so much better. People have died and others have been born and die in their millions throughout the ages, and the way of life is in death. We shouldn't love each other individually too much, since the last parting between loved ones, the living and the dead, is so very painful. We should love all and in this way our sorrow will lessen when the individual loved one departs. Death is too terrible for us to bear even though our sorrow, our torment, our helplessness.

I announce news of death and absorb within myself the shock and terror of the death blow to those who remain alive. I can't save a soul. Maybe by being the announcer, I sustain them a little. Each day I become more and more devoted to this work. Not that I find it holy, but it does give me the ability to bring a little cheer and to ease the pain of my villagers. I'm the man who summons the doctor to declare someone officially dead, who rounds up the burial society, the grave-diggers and those who chant psalms. At the set hour, I circulate among the shroud sewers, the coffin-makers, grave-stone cutters. Except for the nursery of carnations I keep, it's been long since I farmed, and I spend much time caring for the cemetery that slopes down from our village. I planted a pretty little garden to death down there. Cypresses, pine trees, oaks, willows; clipped grass, flower beds carefully kept. Many an hour I roam about there with my hoe and clippers and watering hose. I cut the grass, I crumble the earth in the flower beds and dust the marble tombstones. In time, the village council on its own allotted me a permanent salary for my work, and it was sufficient for my household and me. Yes, many an hour I exhaust myself laboring in the cemetery, and only when I suddenly imagine that I'm enjoying it, do I rise, gather my tools and leave.

In the village people are beginning to fear me a little. Somehow they're careful not to look at me as they walk by. They avoid my eyes by looking down as they pass me. It seems that something of the mark of death has stuck to me, and even though no one here believes in old wives' tales, nevertheless the secret of all fears in the world is that first and last fear, the giant of all fears: fear of this terrible and frightful death. Everyone dreads it. Only I am not afraid of death.

4

Yes. I'm not afraid of death. I've already completed the circle of my life even though it still lingers on awhile. I know that what I'm saying is strange. Most people avoid thinking about their death, unless one longs for it as my wife does. But everyone else inwardly flinches from it, pushes it out of his thoughts. As for myself, I reflect on my dying day very calmly. Even if suffering awaits me, I'm not afraid. No, I'm not crazy, so I don't force the issue. Nevertheless I'm ready for it. I also yearn to return to my twin brother, who died soon after he was born, to see if he's really waiting for me there. I think about the day I'll join him and my father. I know its unnatural, but despite this, I'd like all those I love — nine hundred and seventy-three men and women, aged, boys and girls, children and infants, all my fellow villagers — to also contemplate their deaths freely, peacefully and in quiet, like the death of a stranger, of someone else; without primitive fear, without panic. Maybe that way, when it does come, our torments will lessen. The solitary terror of death will be painful, and the sorrow will be divided among the whole community, everyone with his small share so that the portion of pain is not so burdensome as when borne alone. Maybe my thoughts are mad, but they may also serve the general good: to calm this one and to give rest to that one, something that doesn't exist elsewhere. I'm always trying to find ways to make people happy.

Because of this, about five or six years ago, I decided to act. One day I regretted what I had done to that man Beno, her husband, to his children, to my wife, Yota, to the people of my village, and I tried to bring things back to the way they once were. I wanted to return Yota to her family. I wasn't her family. I still loved her then and at times she still desired me. Nevertheless I wanted to do good. I was conscious stricken over my sin. One evening I went out and knocked on his door. I wanted to tell that thin, neat, well-combed man, whose existence was so miserable, that the torment I suffered over the wrong I had done him was far greater than his own wretchedness. Maybe, as others do, he'll find some consolation in that. I wanted to say that I was ready to end everything. Let his wife return to him and I'll never see her again. I can make out on my own.

I stood in the dimness of the doorway, my back to our lovely village night and I said what I had to say. His daughter, her face pale, looked at me and he pursed his lips and laid down his newspaper. I know how much he loved his wife and how much he had been tormented until this day at what we had done. I don't remember the words I chose. I was leaning against the door, perplexed though determined, careful that my boots wouldn't dirty the clean floor. He lowered his gaze, still unable to look me in the eye as if he was to blame, and I looked directly at him to absorb all his pain, a punishment equal to my sin.

He remained quiet for what seemed a long time. "I think," he finally said slowly and perturbed, spreading his fingers and studying them. "I think not. What's the sense. You understand?" He lingers over his words, turning to his daughter. "Time, as they say, did its work. That is, we learned —" his eyes still observing his daughter with quiet love. "We've learned to surmount our — what happened. We learned without her. It was difficult for me." He nods his head to himself. "For the children. Very difficult. Yes." Again he studies his fingers, stops and remains silent for a long time. It's harder than hell for him to talk to me. "But it's better the way it is now. What I mean is the years have passed. You can't start all over." He searches for words. "To try again. It can't be as before. And if it's not as it was before —" Now he lifts his eyes to me for the first time in his life and they are bright and wise, somewhat mocking; a belated victorious glint shines from them. I didn't come to argue with him, having given in even before I dared to step across the threshold; surrendered to the eyes of the man whom I carried long ago, bleeding from his attempted suicide to a life of humiliation. "— what's the sense of it?" he finishes his sentence.

"Listen," I say to him in my brash unclear way. "You loved her. Lots. I know. She was a very pretty woman. She still isn't bad." Their city, Kovno, flashes before my eyes: gray houses and a boulevard faced with dark leaved trees, and she and he, young as in a painting, her thin gloved hand holding a parasol, her thin figure in a blue dress and she desiring him, and her yellow hair blowing in his face. For they had once known days of love, and yearned for each other at night. Didn't she leave her own land and follow him? Abandon her whole world for the madness of his other native land where their lives would be separated and ruined? Back there they probably wouldn't have known any sorrow. "Listen," I say. "This whole business, I was just a dumb kid. I know. It's not worth going over all that. Believe me. I'm very sorry. All the time. It's been a year, maybe longer, that I've been thinking of coming to you and until now I just — you understand — I couldn't find the courage. Every night I drive myself to come and then I retreat." I wipe the sweat off my brow. "I know. It's not proper for someone like me, one who did what I did, to come and talk with the one he did it to —" I stop, then continue. "I — I can't help it. I can't. Because —" Again I'm stumped for words. I look at him and he purses his lips and lowers his eyes again. But he's more stubborn than I am, more determined. I know. His daughter remains quiet. Her hair is fair and long like her mother's. Her face is narrow and delicate and her eyes are soft like her father's. Her animosity shows itself in silence or maybe she's confused. Her brother is in the army and during his leaves, when he strolls through the villàge, he avoids me. I never had children and he, her son, is handsome and I would have liked him as a son. We never exchanged a word since that time when he was still a boy and he came to get me to help his father whose wrists were slashed.

I plead with her husband in the dim-lighted doorway. "Listen. She's sorry. She cries at night," I say, avoiding his daughter's eyes, and with as much refinement as I possess, I say curtly, "It's three years that I . . . almost. She keeps away from me. What I mean is nothing happens anymore. You understand? I don't ask a thing from her. Both of us regret all this and at night —" But he angrily cuts me off with a hand whose strength I had never suspected. "Enough!" he declares uncompromisingly.

But I try again. "She cries at night. She's sorry. People do foolish things sometimes. I know. Even terrible things are done. But it's possible to correct them. She's miserable. Very miserable. Why should she pay for one mistake all her life?" And I'm about to say to him that maybe in me, the animal, big and powerful, she had instinctively thought, frightened, alien and torn from her past, that she would find the salt of this land to which she was brought. Maybe that's the way it was — the root of it all. Who knows? Except for her moments of joy and her torments, I never really knew her. "She hardly eats anything," I say. "She roams the house like a shadow. Never goes out. And when she lies down at night, she turns her head to the wall."

He stands up looking coldly and fiercely at me. "Enough!" he says. "Everyone pays for his mistakes and not every mistake can be corrected." He looks at me angrily, and his words are ordered as if he had planned them many days before. His daughter remains silent. "You," he hisses at me, "have no concept how miserable we were. We learned to live with our misery. To walk with it amidst those cursed, pitying looks of your villagers; with the graciousness and goodness and compassion of your protectors. We learned to be seen and not see. To lock ourselves up in our house. To forget," he laughs joylessly. "Yes, to forget."

He stops smiling. "There were days and nights of vengeful thoughts. Yes, I haven't slept at all since then. I'm a phenomenon." His eyes flash. "Did you ever hear of a man who hasn't slept in fifteen years? I lie at night and think about both of you. And during my work," he continues, his eyes flashing brighter, "I do my work like a machine. The calculations are worked out by themselves, without error. I'm a phenomenon. You're on my mind all the time. Always. You and she. She and you. All the time. Afterward I no longer think of revenge. I'm tired of vengeance. I want peace from my seething thoughts and there's no relief. Only slowly, without sleep, without rest, the pain eases a little. Nothing is forgotten, my friend," he quickly warns me. "But in reconciling myself to all this, a quiet comes. There's no longer any room in our lives for new storms, my friend." He looks at his daughter. "She's sixteen now. Soon she'll begin her own life. She's already adjusted to our way. I won't burden her now with that woman. She knows all, understands everything. Right?" His daughter nods slowly. "There's no place here for forgiveness and retribution," he spits out. "The whole business is over. Nothing can change."

I walk to my house through the darkness, back then, a few years ago, I knew that he still loved his wife dearly as much as he hated her. I can't do a thing for them. I can't. From now on her life will flicker out slowly before my eyes.

Time helps a little. After two or three years, I convince her son Uri's young wife, a sweet girl from our village who understands my pleas, and she brings the daughter, Iza, before she leaves to do her army service, to see my wife. After a while the son also comes. I'm glad that he married one of the village girls. In the next generation all this will be forgotten. From time to time her children knock on the door, enter, their faces expressionless, ask for their mother and then close themselves in together. They have nothing to say to me. For my wife these are hours of pitiful joy. Her husband, Beno, knows all this and glowers at me because I succeeded a little. I bear him no grudge for this. I'd like to make up to him as well, but I don't know how. He's a proud man and I'll never succeed in making him forget how deeply I hurt him.

A year ago her daughter-in-law brought the first grand-child over, and my wife's eyes widened with admiration as she lay on her bed. She held the infant, caressed him and called to him as out of a far away and hidden dream: "Stefan. Stefan."

"But Yota," protested her daughter-in-law — I was allowed to stand at the door — "his name is Ayal. Ayal!" This other name didn't even raise a glint in her eyes. For her he was Stefan. Maybe it was then that I realized that she wouldn't last much longer. In these past few days, I'm preparing myself for her death. I leave her side only when her heavy breathing subsides and her face softens. I know then that she's sleeping. It's been weeks now that she suffers listlessly from some unknown disease. The kindly village doctor gives her bottles and small packets filled with pills, but she refuses to take them. I don't urge her. I see death in her eyes. I've already notified her children and they came and stood frozen before her bed. When she opened her eyes and saw her grandson, she burst into rasping cries and a bad cough. The year old infant became frightened and his own crying quaked in harmony with the grandmother's sobs. Until now the son, the daughter, the daughter-in-law were her only visitors. Occasionally a kind neighbor would come in, either out of curiosity or compassion, in order to help clean the house. Her husband, Beno, suffers from rheumatism and for the past few months has taken to using a metal cane. He's a proud man and refuses to see her. In her delirium and pain, was she expecting him to come? I don't know.

When they all get out finally, I rise from my armchair in the next room leaving my newspaper and book, and go and look at her. I have no love for you, my Yota, strange, unfortunate, Gentile. I have much compassion for you. I understand your sickness and I know why you're dying. If I wasn't what I am, I would try, after you die, to have your body returned to your city, Kovno. When you open your eyes, the mist at times rises from your lids, and through the fever, you recognize me at your bedside, and you scream with fear. Occasionally, in the rain, against a pale winter sunset coming through your window in the gloaming, I imagine I hear you cursing me and my village. We are your nightmare, your bad dreams, and there's no consolation in those few memories we shared. You will die and you will be granted more honor in your death than when you lived. The whole village will come to send you off to that other world, and the sorrow of your death will be divided, each one taking a share of it. I will mourn your wretchedness quietly, while hundreds of people will pass through the gates of my green and lovely cemetery which is ringed with cypresses. They will come to it across the seven roads leading to my village, through its grasses, its flower beds, and they will stand silently and watch as you are lowered into the grave.

Translated by Daniel Spicehandler

The Terrible Tale of Josef de la Reina

DAN TSALKA

Josef de la Reina was a great man, wise in the ways of practical Kabbalah. He lived in Safed, in a modest hut across from Mount Canaan.

One evening when he was nine years old, he heard the tale of the aged scholar who had summoned forth Samael with adjurations. The elder had sealed a pact selling his soul and Samael had become his servant. De la Reina told himself that he too would learn the oath, call forth Samael, kill him and remove all impurity from the world. Then all mankind would say: greater than all was Josef de la Reina. He never thought of himself but battled the king of evil to become pleasing to God and to bring the Redemption. De la Reina marveled that nobody had ever done this; that this deed, most important of all, was not spoken of constantly. However, when he saw the confusion or grins of those to whom he turned, de la Reina hid his desire, revealing it only to his teacher Tuvia Rosa, known to those in Safed as the "mad Italian."

De la Reina studied day and night and already in his youth was renowned not only in his home town but also in Tiberias and in Jerusalem. As his views were unconventional he had to leave his home; for he hated the corruption of the

family, sermons before small crowds and even the smugness
with which a man turned to his spouse on strolls through
the streets. He went to live in that wretched hut opposite
Mount Canaan and those in Safed began to recoil from his
presence.

One day his teacher Tuvia Rosa felt his death approach.
He called de la Reina to himself and said: "With unequaled
munificence God permitted man to be whatever he desires.
Animals — the moment they are born they are as they will
be at death. The Higher Creations, angels and cherubs —
from the moment of creation their nature is eternal. Only to
man was given every chance. That which he nurtures will
mature. If he cultivates his vegetative nature — he will
become a plant; his animate — an animal. If he develops
wisdom, understanding and compassion — he will become as
the angels. And if he is displeased with the fate of the
created he will be gathered to the center of darkness and
there become one without end. Thus must man do, and no
more. Forget your desire and go to the holy Rabbi Isaac
Luria, the Lion, who currently is pleased to speak with
pupils and to pray in their company. Promise me!"

De la Reina promised this to his teacher who, as death
approached, taught him all he knew of Combinations,
Unities and Intentions, not withholding a thing.

"Forget your desire," he told him in sorrow.

"I must kill Samael," answered de la Reina.

Even though de la Reina shrank from contact with the
townspeople and their scholars, he kept his promise and one
day descended to Nahal Amud, where Luria sat with his
disciples. Nahal Amud was filled with sprightly flowing
waters and pools alongside which grew shade giving plane
trees, graceful weeping willows and tiny willows. Coming
from the sterility and dryness of the hills, de la Reina was

pleased at the humidity and the murmur of cool waters. Under the curved branches of the plane tree, surrounded by waters, he saw the Sacred Lion, dressed in white clothing, sitting with his disciples as if on a tiny island, his feet dangling in the waters. From every corner of the wadi rose the pleasing odors of arbutus and mint, of cardamom and river berries.

"Sit with us, de la Reina," spoke the Sacred Lion, indicating a spot next to him and offering a basket of black berries. De la Reina lived alone in a humble cottage and was unaccustomed to conversation. Both tall and hunched, his features shrouded, he sat amidst the group and mainly through discomfort, heard nothing. Nonetheless, he was impressed by Luria's appearance, surrounded by disciples hanging on to every word from his mouth and looking on with devotion. He was taken also with Luria himself, with his handsome head and pleasing voice.

After a week de la Reina returned to the same place. Again Luria invited him to sit at his side and again the disciples unwillingly made room for him.

De la Reina saw and listened to their words and to the whisper of two streams circling the island and looked at the flowing waters in which the branches of the plane tree were reflected. Fixing his stare, he saw suddenly darkness descend on the trees, on the mountains, on the streams and that in the dark were not two streams but rather two parts of a huge beast which ascended above the hills to the skies themselves. The sun reddened and the two paws of the animal rose higher and higher and even the Sacred Lion and his disciples were no longer pure and unsullied in their finery but were like wooden images, eyes of hollow glass, kneeling on the ground, worshiping the giant beast.

When he saw this sight a terrified scream escaped his

mouth. He ran to his hut sobbing and wringing his hands. From that day, de la Reina made little contact with others and lived in his hut alone. An old woman came once in a while and brought a bit of food. Even though the hut stood far from the houses, there were those who told of strange voices cleaving forth from it and once when he was asleep, they came and spread ashes on the floor of the hut to see if rooster tracks would appear, those being the tracks of devils.

De la Reina was not yet twenty but when he passed children threw rocks and women averted their glances. He feared that they were following him. He would leave the hut, walk around and examine the low roof. Before going to sleep he would check to see if someone was behind the window or under the bed.

With one man only did he associate. His name was Natale Natali. He lived in Vicenza, searching the philosopher's stone, Natali had numerous books on alchemy and magic. De la Reina sent him many letters, requesting various mixtures and telling of his discoveries. He sent him a diary; followed his advice. To him de la Reina confessed his desire to capture and kill Samael. He asked about many things, especially about the mighty kingdom of Spain and its king who ruled half the world; about Avila the city of eighty towers, unbreakable gates, massive bridges, a city of solemn gray stone.

Natale Natali, old and embittered, had no friends or relatives. He was happy that in the Galilee lived a young man who wrote him promptly once each month, and he answered all of de la Reina's queries to the best of his abilities although he knew little of those things not connected with his own search. One day de la Reina received a letter informing him that a ship would be arriving in Jaffa with a noble family from Vicenza and that one of the servants would bring him a phial of herbs, an amulet and an ancient parchment, with the aid of which, between midnight and dawn, de la Reina could realize his desires.

De la Reina glanced at the letter in marvel and could not believe what he read. However, as long as he was not yet able to call Samael by himself, he would be happy to do it using the secrets of others. On the designated day he went to Jaffa to wait for the ship. Indeed, at noon anchored at the port was a pretty Venetian ship with purple sails and window wood the color of honey. Porters carried the passengers ashore on their shoulders, laughing and baring their teeth. De la Reina recognized the family from his friend's description, saw the old servant and alongside him, a three-year-old girl holding a parasol in one hand and combing her yellow hair with the other. De la Reina approached the two and saw the girl had large and proud eyes.

At once the family from Vicenza broke up into groups. The more elderly climbed into a carriage awaiting them at the dock. The younger rode horses and the girl was seated on a mule under a canopy. De la Reina received the packet from the servant and asked him the girl's name and he was told that it was Helena.

The convoy proceeded to Jerusalem and de la Reina returned to Safed, opened the parcel, began to fast, and planned that very week to do what he had contemplated doing for years. He wound the amulet around his neck, tasted the herbs, and as instructed in Natali's letter, sat by the window, the parchment before him, and waited. From the window could be seen the slopes of Mount Canaan, stunted trees, a few shepherds' huts, smoke rising from a bonfire. At midnight he uttered the spell his friend had sent.

Slowly the letters began to stand out from the parchment; their borders wavered and sharpened and rose in a variety of hues. Through the humble room blew a gust of wind which rattled a broken chair and a hanging wooden beam. De la Reina's heart pounded mightily, a hot fever overtook him, the tips of his fingers were as though pricked with thousands of tiny needles; the parchment dispersed slowly, frothing like foam.

De la Reina rose to wash his burning face but before he could even dampen his fingers the water in the barrel itself rose to his palms. Sensing his presence, de la Reina, with pale lips and a twist of the head called for Samael. In a corner of the room, bound by myriad strands of light was a form which de la Reina at first thought was a camel or a huge woman. And now he saw that it was a man a head taller than he sitting on a wooden stool, his large knees nearly touching the floor. The head was that of a mighty man and only in the eyes and mouth were there traces of distortion, as if the shape was about to transform itself into a camel or some other large beast. The creature was naked and the strands of light were like copper threads pressed against its skin. De la Reina felt proud and overjoyed at the sight. He broke out into a loud laugh and lit several candles. The creature did not open its mouth but followed de la Reina's movements with his head and waited submissively.

"Are you Samael?" asked de la Reina at last.

"Here am I, Samael, at your command, noble sir," answered the creature.

"You are the King of Evil, the Prince of Darkness, leader of the satyrs and wild birds, of screech-owls and wild jackals? It is you who wears the form of a snake?"

"It is I, Don Josef," answered Samael.

"And now you are in my hands."

"It is so, Don Josef," said Samael in a controlled voice, as if his good manners were struggling with the desire to flinch from unnecessary comment.

This was the moment de la Reina had waited for since childhood. In fact, however, he had not believed it would come about and was not ready. He could not decide what to do. The sight of Samael generated great curiosity within him.

"How did I succeed in trapping you?" he asked.

"In my sleep, Don Josef," responded Samael.

"Do you really sleep?" marvelled de la Reina.

"I sleep, Don Josef," answered Samael, "although not the sleep of the just." After a pause he added: "I am sure that it was a most difficult task to devote all the years of your youth and prime to studies with the sole purpose of entrapping me. I know also of your life in seclusion and I can well visualize your agonies. One of my servants is a great sinner and with but one slip he suffers torment and pain. Yes, I praise your hard labors."

De la Reina knew of Samael's flatteries and was quiet. But at that instant he felt no hatred for the creature sitting passively on the small stool across from him.

"You were His beloved angel and you rebelled?"

"Yes, Don Josef, as you well know," answered Samael.

"You were His loved one and you rebelled? Not only I but all of creation, the skies and the firmament, the winged and the swarming are filled with terror and hate at the thought of you." De la Reina spoke part of the speech he had been preparing for years.

Samael bowed his great head.

"But now I have trapped you and your time has come. Soon the last of the great trumpet shall be heard."

"Sometimes I am amazed," said Samael modestly. "Do

you really believe that what you say will come to pass after you have killed me, Don Josef?"

"How dare you voice such doubts in my ears," raged de la Reina. He raised his hands to Samael's brow and at once drops of blood bubbled forth. Blood also appeared on his legs and hands. His lips turned black and broke out in numerous open sores. The large body strained with effort. From the gloom beyond the window came the shrieks of various animals, as if they were witnessing the death of one of their own. De la Reina tasted blood on his lips, as when he had first licked his wounded lip in his childhood. He lowered his hand.

Gradually Samael's eyes returned to what they were.

"I am very sorry," he said. "It was curiosity which drove me to ask that question."

"You mock me," said de la Reina. "I cannot permit you to mock me."

"Mock you? Don Josef . . . " said Samael in amazement, "I can mock the learned of your city, and even the Holy Luria, who succeeded in inlaying me like an emerald in their fine mosaic. Like the clerks of a king who must sustain a kingdom, they preserve the day. But mock you, whose thoughts from childhood have been on how to kill me, despite great hardship and unpleasant efforts? No and no, Don Josef, you are not among the learned of your city."

"They are holy men," said de la Reina.

"Yes, they are holy men," repeated Samael after him. "When they arrive in the heavens they are received with rejoicing and the angels sing in their honor. As I told you, they preserve creation. Not one of them ever thought to catch me or kill me."

De la Reina was quiet.

"It is true," continued Samael, "that I don't believe you

will do that, Don Josef. The world is large and very full. You won't do a thing to me."

"Turn into an animal," said de la Reina dryly.

"Men are no better than animals," said Samael, "but I am at your disposal. I shall try to become an animal, perhaps an insect or an old toad. But do not suspect me if I fail. I am bound."

As he said this the strands of light trembled and whitened. Samael's eye closed and his nose flattened. His mouth opened briefly and in it gleamed yellow teeth.

"I am not able to do it," he said at last.

"You lie."

"I am sorry, Don Josef," said Samael. "I am not able to do that which you commanded and I note with astonishment that I still live."

"My heart does not embrace you."

"That I understand very well. But why do you not kill me with the strength in your fingers. Wait and do nothing. The rays of light themselves will kill me. Indeed I shall not die at once but only after long agonies, although that fact does not move you at all."

"You talk like a woman," said de la Reina.

"What do you know of women. You know nothing about them at all."

"Do you not fear death?" asked de la Reina angrily.

"Who knows," answered Samael. "Perhaps the towns-people who think you crazy are right. Your dreams are so childish, so baseless. The world is full and you are but skin and bones. Only with difficulty do you stand on your feet. I can see your skeleton. You will be very ugly when dead, de la Reina."

"Monstrous serpent," exploded de la Reina. "Now you open your mouth and spit sulphur and rot. You stick to every

place like a leech and your servants await you like shadows
in the corners of the ways. Death will not suffice for you. I
am sorry that all these years I did not devise fitting tortures
for you . . ." In that vein de la Reina shouted for a long
time and with evident glee.

"Don't get so excited, like an old virgin who finally
found a husband, my dear Don Josef." Samael succeeded in
breaking in during one of de la Reina's pauses to breathe.
"You are young but the stench of your learned body sticks
in my throat like a chicken bone in the tender throat of an
infant. The learned of your town know how to live in the
world but only you, you polluted Spanish or Portuguese
bastard, won't give a minute's peace to anyone. Let me
loose from here, I'm suffocating."

"Bastard, bastard . . . I'll show you, bastard," shouted de
la Reina.

Samael's eyes narrowed slightly.

"I am sorry," he said in a low voice, "for all the words I
said just now. Once I was very handsome, but ugliness
enwrapped me and infused my words against my will.
Perhaps only you, among all men, can see the remnants of
my form and remember what I once was."

"You called me a bastard," said de la Reina, glancing at
the fine creature slouching on the stool.

"I am sorry," said Samael. "We sit here, Don Josef, in
this humble cottage, needing only a small sign from you to
leave and enjoy ourselves on a ship in the wide ocean on our
way to a delightful island. The world is full of islands of
bliss, Don Josef."

De la Reina looked out the window and it seemed that it
had turned lighter, but curiosity made him forget
everything.

"Rumors reached here," he said, "of Captain Colon who,

with the aid of a wonder-bird and a map which miraculously appeared on his table one night, reached the lands of Eden. But that sounds like a children's fable."

"Fable, Don Josef? All that which you said — is true. Captain Colon reached the shores of Eden."

"In a boat? How can that be?" stammered de la Reina. "Who lives on those islands?"

"The creatures of the islands of bliss," said Samael. "All their lives are of joy and happiness. They know no sin and no toil. They understand the tongues of the animals who live with them. Bread blossoms on the trees and the shrubs are heavy with fruit. There is no law and thus no sin. To each — joy without guilt and no man fears death. They play flutes and sing. If you wanted to go there, there would be nothing easier for you to do. I have a large ship in the port of the gentiles, in the city of Sidon, called by the Arabs Sa'ida. We can sail at once, you and I; I know no less of the sea than Captain Colon.

So as not to fall into the trap, de la Reina changed the subject and said: "Did you object, you angels, to the creation of man?"

"Perhaps," said Samael trying to hide a yawn. "I really don't remember those events too well."

In the hut silence reigned.

"Soon will come the end of Samael," said de la Reina to himself. "It is best that I ask him all my questions."

At once he thought of asking about the king of Spain, ruler of all; of the city of Avila; of instruments from wood and copper to measure the paths of the stars; of the future of the child Helena, and even on the meaning of certain biblical passages which he interpreted differently from the great commentators.

"And what does Captain Colon do now?"

"I see Christobal Colon sitting under the shade of cork-tree branches next to a spring bubbling forth from the ground surrounded by most pleasing girls with long hair and garlands of wild flowers and green sprigs on their heads. Near them youths collect the fruits of the earth without crushing the belly of the Mother-of-all-the-living."

"I have much love in my heart for that captain."

"So it is with us all," said Samael. "If you so desire, I can lead you to him."

"Lead me?"

"So I said, lead you," said Samael. "I did not intend to direct, but am rather like a trusty mule who knows how to climb through mountain trails without slipping to the right or the left."

"And what will happen," asked de la Reina, " to that girl named Helena whom I saw at the Jaffa port?"

"They will marry her to the man who shall govern Athens."

"Queen of the Greeks?" said de la Reina, "like she who brought disaster to her people."

"Disaster to her people? Nonsense. Nonsense, Don Josef," laughed Samael. "Merely a pretense for journeys, adventures and wanderings. The Greek elders forgave her everything when they saw her stroll atop the walls of Troy."

"Such is the plot which old men contrive and such is their entertainment," said de la Reina. "It comes from boredom."

"Senility softens," laughed Samael.

"Perhaps she wasn't so beautiful."

"She was very beautiful," said Samael, "and she strolled on the walls so that a Greek arrow might strike her."

When he heard this de la Reina grew excited, but he continued to speak of the elders and expanded on the topic, spellbound by his astute partner, whose lucid analyses and clear facts were always at the ready. With a smile Samael brought forth endless examples of elders who made laws, of righteous judges of many nations. He even told of the color of their eyes and of their ways of speaking and walking. He added that the experience of their lives and their concern for the essence of life was of the sort that should change them to benefactors in de la Reina's eyes. But de la Reina disagreed with Samael and retorted that all their lives the elders were hovering next to death and with their years they were attacked by the madness to become the only living beings — surrounded by sterility and destruction. Madness emphasizes their achievements which then becomes the essence of their existence.

De la Reina expounded on this at length until his glance fell by chance on the table. He saw the letters on the parchment fade, looked out of the window and fainted.

When he woke, he was lying on a pile of sharp stones. Below, in the narrow streets of the town, appeared the first signs of life. At a distance of one hundred paces he saw Samael sitting on a black rock, wiping his face with his paw like a cat. After a second he disappeared.

De la Reina rose and saw that he was on the top of a tall fortress set between walls built of large stones from which sprouted thin yellow weeds.

The air cleared and de la Reina saw tall Mount Meron, the deep channel of Nahal Amud, the quiet fields of the Galilee, and the silvery waters of the Sea of Galilee. He stood without moving and then looked at the spot from which Samael had disappeared, and said, "We shall meet again!" As always there was but one thought in his heart: I must kill Samael. He returned to his hut dragging his feet.

Unlike other men who go off to live by themselves and after a while return to their families and friends, de la Reina remained alone; only infrequently would he go out to bathe in the Sea of Galilee. Once, on returning to Safed, he had seen farmers hurling rocks at a young passer-by whose hands and head flung all about. De la Reina's first thoughts had been that the man's movements were scattered and unnecessary. It would have been better to behave like other people and not arouse scorn or anger. However, glancing at the cruelty of the farmers he had thought that wars and plagues were sent with justice since only fear could penetrate these people's unenlightened souls. A week later he had been startled to find that that same youth, thin and pale, had come to visit. His name was Jonathan, and he spoke in a weak voice and was mostly silent. De la Reina knew the youth was tormented whenever he heard what was to him a cross word. His hands were frozen at the sides of his body.

"How can it be," said de la Reina to himself, "that my words could grate on somebody's ears?"

He began to think about himself and observe himself and, even though he did not cease his searchings and combinations, was like a sick person. Every look directed his way wounded him.

When the youth came again, de la Reina strove to make him feel comfortable, even scrubbing the floor of the cottage three times. The youth's shyness was no longer evident and he spoke at length. To de la Reina's great surprise, the youth began to refute his opinions sharply and grossly basing his words on teachers de la Reina had succeeded in forgetting years back.

As Jonathan continued talking, de la Reina was able to see his soul, and was startled at the vision. The youth's hands chopped at the air with sharp motions. His voice turned hoarse, dominating, full of derision.

As the youth became more venomous, de la Reina told himself: "Either this man is the agent of Samael or else he will never be a good pupil. It is ridiculous to teach anyone who is not ready to serve me."

He evicted the youth from his home and saw how his hands were frozen.

This meeting left a troubled impression on de la Reina. Before he had been happy that nobody knew him. Even the most insignificant rumors from Safed had annoyed him. Suddenly his anonymity angered him and when he heard, by chance, somebody praise other men, his features contorted.

He would say to himself that those of his generation and time were only worse than their predecessors. Happiness left him, the nights during which he sat alone at his table brought him no pleasure. He worked depressed and a few times tried to drink wine in order to be able to continue. The feelings of spiritual exhilaration which accompanied him before, without his knowing it, left. "All is dry and emptiness," said de la Reina to himself.

Very infrequently a few of the learned men of the town would come to visit out of obligation or pity. They would bring him bread, fruit, a few words from the Holy Luria, and by virtue of these short visits would earn their own as well as their families' admiration for themselves.

When they would leave, de la Reina would tell himself: "You know that they are more clever than you and you do not like to hear their discussions, from fear that you might doubt your abilities and desires as well. But what kind of desires are those that collapse because of a few words? You are weaker than an insect, Josef." Then one day he said to himself: "Why do I work so hard and oppress myself without profit? Perhaps I shall never find the right combinations. There is nothing else from which I can amass strength. Why must I live like some lunatic, sick and infecting others, if I do not believe in my own efforts. I shall leave for the sea and jump in the waters." He recalled his interest of past years, but after having seen the limits of its reign, even the steadfast Kingdom of Spain, whose language and banners once pleased him no longer appeared to him as the heir of long-past kingdoms which had left only a few hopes and ruins behind.

At the same time a merchant from Vicenza — Sermonetta — came to Safed. He had heard gossip about de la Reina, who greatly piqued his curiosity. The merchant Sermonetta was dressed handsomely, his beard was styled and trimmed beautifully. One day he came to de la Reina's cottage and said: "Nobody in this town knows both of us, so permit me to present myself to you. In my home town my name is known to all. I have heard of you and have come to suggest that you join me on my sailings."

De la Reina looked at the merchant and observed his fingernails which were well manicured, painted a rose color, and the rings on his fingers. A gem-encrusted stiletto was tied to his belt. A silver necklace hung from his neck. His clothes were sewn from purple and black silk and his shoes were buttoned in a most complex manner.

"I shall go with this man. Perhaps I shall be so lucky as to see the girl Helena. He certainly has heard of the islands of bliss and perhaps has visited one of them," thought de la Reina, and he asked the merchant: "And how is Captain Colon, the beloved of all?"

"Captain Colon?" said the merchant amazed, "he died

fifty years ago. I did not know that that name had also reached a man sunk in mysteries."

"Fifty years ago?" said de la Reina, suspecting that the merchant was one of those stalking him, if not Samael himself in disguise. "Do you know an old man living in Vicenza named Natale Natali?"

"Yes, I saw him once. One morning three or four years ago he was found dead in his room."

From this answer de la Reina realized that the merchant was not trying to trick him and asked: "Is your country as lovely as they say?"

"Join me and see for yourself," answered the merchant.

"How can I pay for the trip?"

"By revealing secrets," said the merchant. "I am bored and there is no spice to my life. I am rich, my children are grown. My wife plays cards with her friends and I have no more patience for mistresses."

"But what good will come to you from knowledge of the mysteries?" asked de la Reina. The man who was surprised at his interest in Colon and wanted to know of mysteries seemed to him strange and ludicrous.

"I am jealous of those who know," answered the merchant.

"And I am jealous of those who are not me," said de la Reina.

He went with the merchant to Jaffa, where a Venetian ship awaited them; the same ship he had seen years ago, with purple sails and the wood of its windows the color of honey.

The ship's captain stepped forward to receive the merchant. He was a gross man, pleasant, sly as a fox, a criminal look in his eyes, the son of a noble Venetian family. The merchant Sermonetta guided de la Reina to his spacious cabin, and his servants unloaded rugs and vases from crates and boxes, hand-hammered eating utensils, many-branched candelabra, clocks decorated with the images of heroes. The voyagers were happy that their visit to the Holy Land had ended and that they were returning home with souvenirs and stories.

Those of the large group, who had gone with the captain for two weeks, tried to approach individual pilgrims and members of the smaller groups. Each listened to the tale of the other and tried to remember it.

But de la Reina looked with great jealousy upon those who occupied the ship: heroes and hermits and merchants and cripples. On the lower deck sat a woman, her legs spread out before her, her hair coarse like rope, painting her thin white lips, toothlessly smiling as she looked into an oval mirror. She drank from a bottle of wine and with her feet tried to wake a man lying supine and snoring next to her. De la Reina was jealous even of her, and of the ship itself — a large and fancy plaything — of sea-gulls, of the sea, of everything. "Even my curiosity to see Helena is nothing but jealousy," he told himself.

On the third day of the voyage, the merchant asked when he would begin to reveal the mysteries, and de la Reina answered "tomorrow," but that night he dreamed a dream.

In his dream he saw a small valley with numerous ruins, set between chalk mountains. The sound of howling dogs rose out of the ruins. De la Reina knew that a terrifying creature, a vicious animal or highwayman, wandered among the ruins, ambushing its victims and slaughtering them. Despite this, he proudly entered the valley in hatred of the blood-thirsty creature. Around him he heard cries, groans and sounds of chewing. Without hiding he stood among the ruins, relying on an agreement. This agreement indeed existed, but only within himself. However, de la Reina imagined that it was written in the heavens, that it would bind the vicious being who then could not hurt him. Suddenly he heard a rustling in the bushes: it was after him. Attacked by great fear, de la Reina began to run. Dodging through the paths, in narrow crossings, he descended to channels and pits and ascended the sloping walls of the valley. He ran through huge fields and dark lanes. His only thought was to be saved, his lungs aching, his saliva salty and bitter in his mouth. That sprint brought him to a small ruin from which the edge of the valley could be seen. He saw that he was not fleeing alone: preceding him was a whole group of people who ran much faster than he.

At that moment in his dream de la Reina knew that soon he would be torn apart by the creature. He stopped and hid behind a rock. Despite ducking his head as deeply as he could, he knew that it stuck out from behind the rock. He thought of the agreement and then knew that the creature indeed was a party to it, that a mocking grin was on its lips and that its eyes looked around. De la Reina saw all that in a flash as the creature slithered at his side, its grin sardonic, its eyes blinking and its voice like a stifled laugh. De la Reina also saw the heads of several of his townspeople and immediately his face was covered with a strange and mysterious wisdom. The heads disappeared and again the sound of wailing and grinding was heard.

Memory of the moment the creature had glided to his side came back to de la Reina, his heart was gripped with an embarrassing fear, and he turned his mysterious features towards the townspeople. This memory brought a cry to his sleeping lips. He could not wake up, hard as he tried, and he continued in his dream to stand behind the rock, his look fixed on the edge of the valley and the nearby lake filled with turbid, muddy water. From above de la Reina glanced at the lake when suddenly two sea beasts swiftly rushed out from each of its two sides. When they approached one another, one swallowed the head of the other, and the head ate the belly that had swallowed it and both beasts disappeared below the lake. The water moved a bit and a large blood stain appeared on it and again there was movement at the corners of the lake and again two sea beasts came forth, drew near and devoured each other, and their black spines and white stomachs churned in the terrible waters.

Despite all his efforts, de la Reina could not wake up. His vision returned time after time until he told himself in his sleep: when I wake up I shall jump in the water as I have decided. I have nothing to do in Vicenza or indeed in any other place.

As soon as he awoke, before dawn, de la Reina slipped onto the deck and jumped into the sea. His mouth filled with salty water, his lungs could no longer breathe and he sank deeper and deeper until he fell unconscious.

When he opened his eyes he was sitting on a small rowing bench in a flat boat that was in a puddle of water.

Across from him sat a strange sea monster, its whole body transparent and dripping, filled with thin veins. Its eyes seemed painted on and only its mouth appeared human, as if at any moment it would turn into the mouth of an ass. The monster rowed serenely with two transparent flippers and chattered or hummed a tune to itself. Far off were the shores of a calm island and rows of tiles on the roofs of fishermen's homes. As soon as the creature saw that de la Reina had opened his eyes he said to him:

"Let me tell you something, Josef de la Reina. You are

the first man for whom I have toiled like some slave from the Barbary Coast. Your voyage proves the degree of your stupidity. You arrived only when you sniffed a bit of emptiness. By the way, Helena left Vicenza a long time ago. But to jump into the water . . . Josef, we don't want you to disappear among the waves just as soon as you have begun to learn a little lesson."

De la Reina looked at the ludicrous and repulsive creature and was seized with severe sea sickness.

"Who are you?" he asked.

"An old joker like you," said the creature, splashing a bit of water on de la Reina with one flipper while mumbling to itself.

"All this is hallucination," said de la Reina to himself. "I did not wish to be saved and I did not request to meet anyone."

"Of course it's an illusion" murmured the creature in a soothing voice.

Everywhere the fins of the creature touched, de la Reina saw the bodies of fish, their bellies white and bright and their mouths gaping.

"Leave this boat, evil monster," said de la Reina.

"Evil monster . . . !" said the creature greatly affronted and with complaint in its voice. "There is no gratitude in your heart, Josef de la Reina. Everybody would be enraged if they heard the tone of voice with which you address your savior. Not only do I work hard, but I even sit squeezed in the end of the boat so I can row with both flippers and bring you to shore faster."

"Let me die," said de la Reina.

"Not after two days of rowing and being so near this lovely shore," said the monster. "Within, Josef de la Reina, you have had great faith and yet when you are confronted with a bit of void the tears begin. Long live Perdition, I want to die, leaps from ships at night. No, no, Josef, this isn't the proper time. Your years of solitude have made it impossible for you to disappear under the water so easily."

De la Reina groaned.

"Why do you suffer? Everything will be as it has been until now, if not worse. Relax, there is no end to things," said the monster and coquettishly splashed a bit of water at him.

"It pains me greatly," it added, "that you don't know how to talk."

"My God, my God," moaned de la Reina.

"In my opinion these silences, these jealousies, are the reason for all disasters. Open your mouth, gabble a bit. Exchange words. Words have no meaning, no one intends anything. So show me you know how to talk. It's true that you're wet and thirsty, but still you could say something. I swear to you, have a little fun with me, de la Reina."

Again de la Reina became sea sick.

"Pay attention," said the monster as if it were about to grab his head. "Pay attention to the great difference between land and sea. It's not nice that everything moves. I see you hold your body as if your limbs were about to fly off every which way."

"I want to die," whispered de la Reina when he saw the boat swiftly approach the shore.

"You'll die when we're done with you, you despicable creature," said the monster angrily. Its entire transparent shaking body darkened and crumbled before de la Reina's eyes.

The fisherman who saved him cared for him for several weeks, until consciousness returned and with it, the will to live. The fisherman's family was large, with many children, relatives and children of relatives. De la Reina observed their simplicity and when speaking to them was careful not to hint in any way that he was a stranger who could arouse their yearnings. The head of the family he believed, was a simple and dull man, and he was happy the man was unenlightened.

After a number of months de la Reina sailed to Jaffa and one night arrived in Safed. After his long illness and his long stay on the poor island, de la Reina was glad to see his city. The slopes of the mountains were covered with poppies and tulips, the walls around the houses were whitewashed, the houses clean and whole, the cows and goats contented and the ways well-tended.

He found the city especially pleasing in the early morning hours, before it was heated by the sun, hours when the city was still fresh and washed. He weeded the grass on the floor of his cottage. Without his knowledge, his arrival had aroused the old curiosity and hatred. Transient moods come from man's short life.

He would lie in his bed for long stretches, half-asleep, smelling the leaves of his mattress, his shrouded features showing resignation and exhaustion. He would lie thus for entire days, his glance fixed on the wall. When he first left for town, he went to his teacher Rosa's wife, who was still alive, brought her a pail of well-water and chopped some wood for her. But one night he resumed his search. Indeed, he still worked out of his loathing for man, but was not consistent in these thoughts, for at certain hours of the day or night he heard the rustling of hidden wings.

One evening he heard a knock on his door and a youth entered. He was of medium height and stood erect. His eyes were quick and his thin lips showed great impatience. Patches of beard sprouted here and there on his face.

"My name is Yehuda Meir," he said, looking at de la Reina in adulation. "I want to be your disciple."

"I have to think about that," answered de la Reina. "Come back in a month."

The youth bowed and left. During the month de la Reina met a few other youths, who looked at him with expectation and curiosity.

Thus thought de la Reina: "The forces of the camp of darkness are so great that they seem to fill all existence and besides them is nothing. They are prepared and their laws steadfast, and here I stand alone, having lost the sources of my strength long ago. In all those years in which I studied the mysteries, I never asked for aid from anyone. But perhaps had I chosen man instead of solitude, continued the combinations which I had stopped before my voyage, and preserved all the axioms which I had received from my teacher, I could turn to the supreme angels and the camps of the seraphs and the saintful and request their aid."

He decided to accept disciples and received five, the youngest being Yehuda Meir. I do not know the names of the others as they are not mentioned any place.

De la Reina taught them all that was necessary, for he was ready to use every means and every fellow creature in the heavens or the earth to reach his goal. He was very stringent about all the rules and the crowd of disciples did not diminish his fervor.

Thus passed four years.

One day de la Reina knew that the time had come. He called together his disciples and said: "My sons, I gave my heart to explore and seek out wisdom, so as to bring satisfaction to our creator and to remove corruption from the earth. I feel that I must make haste lest I be swallowed up in the slumber of days. But this is a hard path and from it, perhaps, there is no return."

All the disciples answered: "Our father and teacher, we are ready for whatever you command of us, for God is with you and we are your servants and disciples." De la Reina knew that they desired danger because of their youth and so warned them again. But the disciples stood fast.

De la Reina told them: "If so, purify yourselves and change your garments. For three days do not go near a woman and prepare provisions for we leave here on the third day and we shall not return until we conquer the King of Evil."

On hearing these words, the disciples rose in haste, washed, and dressed in clean clothes. For three days no woman touched them. When they were ready, they went to de la Reina's cottage and as he was not there they went to the house of study. De la Reina sat there in abstinence and purity, his head between his knees. At their coming he raised his head and said: "Come with me, my sons. May it be so that the Shekinah suffuse our deeds."

And they all answered: "Amen. May the will of God bring success to your hand."

De la Reina took many kinds of spices and herbs and writing implements and at sunset ascended Mount Meron with his disciples. They prostrated themselves on the grave of Rabbi Shimon bar Yohai. On the grave grew sharp thorns and around it protruded sharp stones, but de la Reina stretched himself out on the grave all night. His disciples too snatched only a few winks of sleep.

It was a black night, without moon or breeze. De la Reina closed not an eye and only towards morning drowsed a bit. In his dream he saw two men dressed in blue and knew that they were Rabbi Shimon bar Yohai and his son Rabbi Elazar. The two drew near and sat one foot away from him.

"You have taken an onerous task upon yourself, de la Reina," said Rabbi Shimon with restraint. "Be careful! Guard your soul."

"Is my intention desirable?" asked de la Reina.

"It is if you succeed," answered Rabbi Shimon, who looked at the disciples with sorrowful eyes and disappeared with his son. De la Reina spoke to them in his dream: "The Lord knows my suffering and will help me for the honor of His hallowed name. Please return to me, Rabbi Shimon, and you, Rabbi Elazar, and honor me with your advice."

But the two did not return. De la Reina lay with his eyes closed until rays of the sun struck his face. He then rose and went with his disciples to a dense forest near Tiberias.

They sat fasting all day in the forest, seeing neither man nor beast, but only the fowl of the heavens. They combined the Holy Names and mysterious unities which were known to them. Then they went to immerse themselves in the Sea of Galilee and directed a special combination of names to each dipping. Thus they passed three days in fasting, immersion and combination. At night they ate no meat and drank no alcohol or wine.

Towards evening de la Reina and his disciples rose and prayed with great intensity and at the places where the Ineffable Name was expressed in terms of His Lordship, they would pronounce the Great Tetragrammeton as it is written, with punctuation known to them and with the required unities. With long prayer and great adjurations they implored the supreme angels by the power of the Name to raise up Elijah the Prophet to come to them at once, speak to them and instruct them what to do and to give reality to their thoughts.

They waited with bated breath, de la Reina's head lifted to the heavens and the disciples crowded about him.

As they finished the prayers they fell to the ground. Suddenly the prophet appeared from the air and twice beating his rod on the ground, said: "I have now come unto you. Say that which you request."

De la Reina bowed deeply and did not raise his eyes beyond the edge of the prophet's black cloak. He said: "True Prophet! It is revealed and known to our Lord that not for myself have I disturbed you, but for Him. I implore you: show me the path by which I may conquer the Other Side."

At this the prophet answered: "Know this, de la Reina: that which you are about to do is too onerous for you and cannot be done, for Samael and his following are greatly strengthened by the many sins of men. If you wish to struggle with him you must increase purification, dedication, and self-mortification. If not, he will strike you and harm you."

"Is my intention desirable?"

"It is if you succeed. But that is a hard task and thus I advise you: desist yourself, for Samael and his followers will harm you."

At this de la Reina responded: "Do not weaken my hands, True Prophet, but strengthen me and grant me courage, for I am sworn not to return to my home until I fulfill my intention. Instruct me what to do and I shall dedicate my soul and my spirit to the honor of my Lord."

Upon hearing that de la Reina was prepared to die to achieve his goal, the prophet reversed his opinion and said: "Listen to me, de la Reina. If you are able to do that which I command you this day, good will be your portion and pleasing your destiny."

De la Reina and the pupils again bowed and the prophet said:

"Sit in a field far from any settlement, and avoid man or beast. Remain there twenty-one days without eating and without drinking from morning until night. Let your only sustenance be bread and water and even this bread you shall eat not to satisfy your hunger but only that amount necessary to sustain life. Each night you shall reduce the amount you eat until you are accustomed to eating only a minute portion. You must also become accustomed to inhaling spices, so that your substance be pure and clean, for only thus may you be able to see the heavenly angels. Each day immerse yourselves twenty-one times and at the end of twenty-one days make a hiatus and fast for three consecutive days, day and night. On the third day, following afternoon prayers, recite the Great Name derived from the passage 'Above Him stood the Seraphim,' as you know it, punctuated as in the source. At that moment cover your faces and entreat by the Hallowed Names that the angel Sandolphon come to you, he and his followers. When they come, strengthen yourselves at once with a good scent for fear and trembling and weakness will fall upon you at the sound of their approach. At once throw yourselves to the earth and recite the Name in a loud voice. Sandolphon will say to you: 'Why did you do such a deed?' And you, when you hear him speak with resounding voice, your spirits shall flee and you will remain powerless, as if dumb, and you will not be able to answer at all. Beseech him and plead that he give you strength to speak and he will tell you what to do for he is guardian of the ways and paths lest Samael enter the holy sites. He knows all the stratagems of Samael and those places in which he becomes strengthened. Care for yourself, de la Reina, and take heed, you youths."

As he said this, the prophet faded above the tree-tops.

De la Reina and the disciples rejoiced in the prophet's words and did that which he commanded. They sat in a large field yellowed from heat. They mortified themselves and thought not of this world but only of axioms and mysteries of the Chariot until their material substance was nearly made spirit. At the end of the designated days they arose in great awe, covered their heads and prayed with great intensity. In place of the Tetragrammeton they recited the Great Name as it was written and punctuated and in harmony and melody known to them shouted with all of their strength: "Hear us, O Lord of the Chariot."

And when their shouts ceased, the heavens opened and suddenly Sandolphon the angel and all his host came to them in chariots of fire and horses of fire. Great tongues of flame filled the earth and a great quake was heard in the world, and de la Reina and his disciples were most afraid.

They fell on the ground in terror, but fortified themselves with the odor of frankincense which they held in their hands. Despite this, they remained weak and could not speak.

Upon seeing them lying thus, helpless, the angel spread out his great wings and said:

"Sons of Men, best that you sit in your homes lest my legions harm you and immolate you with the vapor of their breaths."

De la Reina moved his lips voicelessly until, overcoming, he said: "My Lord, Angel of God! I tremble before the great fire. Strengthen me and grant me courage and permit me to speak before you."

"Speak," said the angel.

De la Reina looked upon his disciples, who were still unable to rise, removed his shoes and said: "Peace be upon you and on your coming, angel of the Lord of Hosts, and peace be upon all you hallowed legions. Aid me, for I do this not for my honor nor the for honor of my father's house, but for the living God! Aid me, you and your legions. Show me the way to eliminate Evil from the world. Tell me how I can lower Samael from his dwelling place and raise up the hosts of the hallowed."

"Your words are good," answered the angel. "Let God be with you. The ranks of the seraphim and the holy are sitting and awaiting God's revenge and the rule of the avenged Shekinah. But now, son of man, all which you have done until now is but nothing, and if you only knew the status of Samael you would not have become involved in this matter, for who other than God is his equal in strength? Even I myself know not the strength of his forces and only two angels, Akatriel and Metraton, know of the ebb and flow of his powers.

"I know," said de la Reina, "how small I am but my desire is most strong. Teach me what to do to call down Akatriel and Metraton and by which Name I might conjure them. Let me die but I must see the face of the hallowed angels so that I merit eternal life."

His words pleased the angel who approached him. De la Reina looked at his disciples but they still lay on the ground without voice. The angel taught him of the snares of Samael and how to avoid them and when he finished his words the sound happiness was heard in his camp and at once the angel disappeared, lightning striking from his chariot, a long tremulous noise freezing the air.

De la Reina raised up his disciples and led them to a cave on Mount Meron, as the angel had commanded. It was extremely dark and little light entered.

In this cave they spent the time of self-mortification,

abstinence and combinations as commanded by the angel until they were extremely weak and pure and the calm summer air outside the cave seemed to them as sharp as a whip.

One morning a strong wind began to blow outside and a thick brown dust surged up at the entrance to the cave. The wind blew unceasingly and lifted up the plants, sand, gravel, the ground itself, and uncovered black rocks and when everything was stripped bare and black, de la Reina and his disciples left the cave and a constant sterile wind, monotonous and steadfast, wailed in the dryness.

De la Reina told his disciples not to loosen their grips and not to leave the circle — what would be would be and they that tremble would tremble. Thus they stood in the circle and cried to the angels and the more they shouted the more the silence about them deepened. Not even the chirping of birds was heard.

Suddenly the earth shook. With lightning and thunder the heavens opened and the angels descended in blazing chariots which would have harmed them had they not locked their hands. The angels were greatly angered.

"Who is this man," they said, "who is this man who does not fear the angel's specter, mightier than stormy winds, splitting trees and crushing rocks?"

All the heavens dazzled and de la Reina feared that soon the great angels would disappear. He inhaled frankincense, prostrated before them and whispered the words as Sandolphon had advised.

The angels sat on two seats before their chariots, under a star-studded canopy and two lions held the specters in their paws. To de la Reina's whisperings the angels responded with frozen stillness, they and their legions which spread to wherever the eye could reach. Only the rustle of the flames and the beating of the banners was heard and golden shields glittered in the sun.

"Speak up and we shall hear you," said Akatriel.

De la Reina opened his mouth like a dumb fish.

Metraton touched de la Reina's tongue with his scepter and said: "Speak."

De la Reina bowed many times and said: "I implore you, holiest of angels; only one thing is important to me — to uncover the location of Samael and kill him."

"Samael is strong and his force grows. You cannot win. He will strike you and you will die in the twinkling of an eye," said Metraton.

"On my side Samael has a strong barrier: an iron wall from the earth to the heavens," said Akatriel.

"On my side and opposite me," added Metraton, "he has the barrier of a tall mountain of snow whose top reaches to the heavens. You must pass these two barriers to reach Mount Seir."

"Is my intention desirable?"

"If you succeed," answered the angels.

"Will you aid me, holiest of angels?"

Immediately the angels answered, "We will be at Mount Seir and with us will be all your deeds and the likeness of your soul. Every deed which you do below, your soul will do above. Therefore guard yourself and take great care in all your steps."

De la Reina heard their words and the tears fell from his eyes.

"What must I do?"

"Ascend the path which leads up the mountain," said Akatriel, "and if a pack of black dogs approaches you on the way — they were sent by Samael to defeat your intentions. Do not fear them but pronounce the Tetragrammeton to them. From there go and ascend the great snow mountain, careful not to wander from the path, neither to the right nor the left, until you stand facing the iron wall. To pass through it take a knife and slice a doorway in the wall. On the other side you will see Mount Seir. We shall be there. We shall throw down Samael and he will be in your hands. Remember to have with you two lead bands engraved with the Holy Name. You must pursue Samael and his consort Lilith and search them out. They will hide among the ruins and you will find them in the form of two giant black hounds, male and bitch. Approach them without fear and place a leaden collar on each. Fix a rope or chain to their necks and ascend the mountain with them and then the Messiah will be revealed and the whole kingdom will be God's. Remember when they are in your hands they will plead for something to eat. Do not listen to them and give them no sustenance."

The angels mounted the fiery chariots and disappeared in a gale of wind. And there stood de la Reina and his disciples in the great valley at midnight. From each side came the howling of dogs, packs of which came close to de la Reina and his disciples, following them without pause. Their eyes glittered in the dark and their panting filled the air. But de la Reina and his disciples were not afraid and continued on their way. At dawn they came to the mountain of eternal snows and as the sun rose they stood opposite the iron wall, which had no beginning and no end. De la Reina took out the knife, cut an opening and all passed through. On the other side of the wall was a small plain that had several ruins from which came the baying of hounds. De la Reina and his disciples wended their way between the ruins. From the corner of a destroyed hall two giant hounds jumped forth to slaughter them, but de la Reina immediately snapped the lead bands on them and his disciples fixed them to chains.

Once bound the two shed the form of dogs and for the first time de la Reina saw Samael's true image. His wings were double the number of even the holiest angel and he was full of eyes blazing with fire. For a moment de la Reina stood and gaped. Samael gave no sign of recognizing him. Although he had the shape of an angel his head hung low like that of a dog.

They all left the ruins to ascend the mountain, a long and steep path. Samael asked de la Reina for some bread and water but de la Reina did not answer. Towards evening, as it grew colder and a cutting wind whistled by, Samael again turned to him: "My lord," he said, "here we are prisoners in your hands without any strength left. Do as you will, but remember that we were thrown out of our strongholds and without them we have no value, and therefore neither will our deaths. Let us eat and drink something."

"This time you will not leave my hands alive, like the other times," said de la Reina.

"I don't understand," said Samael.

"I know you well," answered de la Reina.

"My lord errs," said Lilith. "Perhaps my lord confuses my husband with someone else. Perhaps it was Asmadeus or some other demon whom my lord encountered."

As she said this, Lilith sobbed, as did Samael. In de la Reina's eyes, it was a terrifying sight to see the proud angel crying and sobbing.

But the disciples rejoiced to see them cry: "Everyone said that our teacher could not succeed, but the heavens will rejoice before this day is done."

Samael heard that and said: "Why is it that you are afraid of me and our legions? We have no strength left at all and we are all in your hands to do as you wish with us. Let us have something to drink before we reach the peak."

De la Reina saw that the peak was no longer far off. Samael's voice was weak and his wings straggled behind.

"Oy, oy, my lord," said Samael, "I am sinking, I die slowly. How terribly are these chains sticking to my body like red-hot irons and the lead bands are even more painful. My body is snow and fire and the fire melts the snow and the snow extinguishes the fire in me. Remove the lead bands, my lord. All creation will wail at my death. The sea will rise out of its bed like milk boiling over; the sun will pale and the stars will leave their orbits, I die, my lord, and all the tortures of hell are naught compared to those I suffer."

De la Reina saw the tears and the suffering of the cursed angel and was not able to endure that sight and that of his disciples holding the ends of the chains in their hands. At each pull the captives trembled and lowered their heads still further.

To fortify himself de la Reina took a bit of frankincense and inhaled.

Samael saw that and said: "Although you give me nothing to drink or eat, at least let me inhale a bit of the frankincense from your hand."

De la Reina stretched out his hand and gave him a bit of the frankincense. At once Samael exhaled a flare of fire from his mouth and singed the spice still in de la Reina's hand.

The smoke rose to Samael's nose and his great wings unfurled.

He rent the chains and tossed the leaden bands from himself and Lilith and stood glowing on the path leading to the peak of the mountain. De la Reina looked up to the peak and saw nothing.

The entire horizon was shrouded by heavy clouds from which rose dense smoke. De la Reina saw two of his disciples fall on the ground lifeless. The faces of two others changed and paled, their eyes goggled and animal shrills came out of their mouths, as if all sanity was ripped from them. Only Yehuda Meir remained, clenching his hands.

De la Reina wanted to approach the two disciples but they began to run away, running, rolling, and laughing a shrill laugh.

De la Reina remained alone with Yehuda Meir, exhausted, astonished at what had happened, for he did not know that the frankincense canceled out the sacred force of the leaden bands. He and his disciple sat next to the two bodies as smoke rose above them.

Suddenly he heard an echo: "Woe unto you, Josef, and woe unto your soul that you did not do that which was commanded you. For you have burnt incense to Samael and he will pursue you to harass you in this world and the next."

As de la Reina heard the echo his features closed and darkened. Without a word he buried the two disciples and then said the *Kaddish* prayer over the graves. The faces of the two others turned green. They wandered from road to road until they returned to Safed where they died from the troubles with which the demons plagued them.

De la Reina and Yehuda Meir also returned to Safed where they were questioned about the fate of the other two, and the police were informed.

That night de la Reina rose, woke his disciple, and the two slipped out of town. After much wandering they came to Sa'ida and as they were very poor and knew nobody there, they rented a room near the port of the Gentiles.

For several months de la Reina kept silent or would

murmur to himself: "In this world and the next!" and would rage at the memory of the echo's words.

As Yehuda Meir earned but little and his teacher was occupied by his own thoughts, the two sat in a room unlit for lack of candles. One evening the landlord entered and said: "Leave here, both of you. I don't want to see you in my house tomorrow."

"Why do you throw us forth from here? Did we not pay you enough and is not winter approaching?" asked Yehuda Meir.

"Winter or no," said the landlord, "you must go. And I don't know what money you're talking about."

"And what is the reason?" asked de la Reina.

"I've reason enough," answered the landlord. De la Reina saw that he was a gloomy man, like a rock surrounded with black grass, and asked, "Do you know any spells against demons?"

"I have nothing to do with demons and I don't need any spell against them like some people," said the landlord.

"Could it be," added de la Reina, "that you do not know Aaron's blessing, the passage from Zechariah and from Psalms, which every child knows are effective against demons?"

"Pack your bags," the landlord said and left.

The same evening de la Reina said to his disciple: "I devoted my entire life to one purpose, without any thoughts for myself. You, dear Yehuda Meir, can testify to that. Yet, despite the great importance of my purpose I suffered from the hatred of my townspeople and their scholars. Although in the end I failed, I stood opposite great angels and their legions and I waged against Samael. It is not just that I should have no share in the world to come. Did you hear the echo, Yehuda Meir, and remember the words:

Your intention is desirable if it succeeds, good is your
portion and your fate. . . . And so, Yehuda Meir, I see that
everything goes its way and that time is nothing but a big
swamp. So I shall go my way. But you, my son, leave me,
and when you hear strange things told about me, remember
who I was and what I did."

To this, Yehuda Meir said: "Please permit me to stay
with you, my teacher."

After much pleading, de la Reina granted his request.

On the same evening for the first time they used the Holy
Names and other names they knew for evil purposes, and at
night robbers came to the landlord, struck him and took all
his possessions. At that point de la Reina began to soil
himself with impurities. He forced demons to bring him all
he desired. He built himself a large house on the beach, after
a time entered into a covenant with the evil Lilith and gave
himself into her hands.

One night Lilith came to him and said, "Good midnight
to you, Josef."

Her maidservant removed Lilith's cloak, stripped her
gown, took off her stockings and shoes and washed her in a
tub which stood in the middle of the room. She anointed
her with fragrant oils and perfumes and around her wrists
and ankles wound small chains of special metal which
increased her charm and her partner's desire. When the
maidservant left, Lilith said to de la Reina: "This is not the
time to stand around pondering, Josef. Come say something
to your little Lilith."

But de la Reina neither moved from his place nor looked
at her. She said: "Just look at me, at your little Lilith."

"Get away from here," said de la Reina.

When Lilith heard this she changed drastically. There was
no man anywhere in the world who would not have

panicked at the sight. Nevertheless, despite the fact that de la Reina was weaker than she and completely in her hands, she remembered the events of Mount Seir and said:

"I know that you've been a bit sad the past few days, so I tried to bring you a gift for which you've waited many years." She removed the image of a beautiful woman drawn in love and exactness from her small red purse.

"Who is that woman?" asked de la Reina.

"Don't you recognize her? That is Helena, the girl you saw in Jaffa seventeen years ago. Tomorrow she will be married to the governor of Athens. Make haste."

When he heard that, fire coursed through de la Reina's body and that very night he ordered the demons to bring Helena to him. Thus he brought her nearly every night to the great bed. At morning the demons would return her.

Yehuda Meir observed all of his teacher's acts. He took no part in the orgies but waited for the day when de la Reina would leave the house on the beach and return to his kabbalistic work. One evening he hinted of his expectation, but de la Reina looked at him angrily and mockingly repeated the echo's words. Only once did he see his teacher sitting at a table at night, head between his hands. In the morning he found a page covered with indecipherable words and mysterious symbols. It was possible to make out only two words: Rosa! Rosa! Yehuda Meir took the page and hid it in one of the walls of the house but never succeeded in removing it again.

One day Helena told her husband: "An odd thing happens to me. Almost every night in my dreams I am taken to a strange place. A man uses me and in the morning I find myself in my bed wet with sperm."

The governor of Athens heard these words and the palace trembled from his anger. He ordered that all the sorcerers in the country be brought to him and commanded them to guard his wife. He told them to prepare spells against the demons and to fix sure traps. The sorcerers did as ordered and one night when the demons came for Helena the sorcerers entrapped them and threw them into a dark prison cell.

"Who are you and who sent you?" asked the sorcerers.

And the imprisoned demons answered: "We are but poor demons sent by Josef de la Reina, who knows all the spells and lives in a large house on the beach in Sa'ida."

At once the governor of Athens wrote a missive to the governor of Sa'ida and asked him to imprison de la Reina and torture him severely. This matter was discovered by one demon who had escaped and he went to warn his master.

Without a word, de la Reina rose and took a boat out to sea. From afar he saw the flickering of a ship's lanterns, but he knew little of seamanship and so sailed further from the shore. The waves pushed the tiny boat into the open sea. De la Reina stood and looked around. From afar he saw the desolate shore of Sa'ida, the deserted port and the dome of the great mosque. The gray waves crashed against the boat and overturned it. They hid his body and crushed the boat as if it had never been. In the morning Yehuda Meir found his teacher's letter which ordered him to flee from Sa'ida, but he did not believe that de la Reina could drown in the sea like any mortal and so went to seek him out. As he returned towards evening he was captured and led off to prison.

In his home town of Safed, much was told about de la Reina's exploits and his sins. They whispered that he had converted to Islam, that an indelible black cross appeared on his back. When rumors of his death reached them, they remembered that he had misled four disciples and was responsible for their deaths. A band of thugs set fire to his cottage, which had been closed up with his mysterious books until that day. Even the holy Rabbi Luria, who was already old and ill, his hands weak and body broken, spoke in the synagogue atop the rock of the fecundity of sin and evil.

As years passed these events were forgotten. The love of the people of Safed for their learned and holy men, and the insatiable curiosity about every detail of their lives, led to the writing of many legends. They were not content with the truth and so would put in the mouths of the great teachers words which had never been spoken. They felt that these words suited them more than those which they had spoken when alive.

Yet among all these stories, the wondrous life and bitter end of de la Reina were not retold.

Once someone wrote two or three pages which did not lack a secret affection. They were written as if by Yehuda Meir, the only survivor, whose location was not known.

Only one young man continued to think about de la Reina. This was Lala Othman, the son of the governor of Athens and Helena. He remembered all he had heard during his childhood and the stories greatly disturbed him. One day he said to himself that when he grew up he would seek out de la Reina's disciple and make him reveal the mysteries.

The youth, Lala Othman, dreamed of the solemnity of responsibility. He was a thorough and precise man who loved tales of sorcery.

On his twentieth birthday, Lala Othman was sent to supervise the supplying of two battalions in Tunis and on his way ordered the ship's captain to dock at Sa'ida.

He put on old clothes and a turban and said that if he did not return within four days the ship should continue on its

way without him. Then, without servants or weapons, he
disappeared into the narrow streets of Sa'ida, sinking in
ancient slumber, flies, and heat. For three days he wandered
the miserable market places and the caravan resting places,
and slept in poor inns. He investigated men, listening to the
conversation of beggars and hermits. But no one had heard
of de la Reina's disciple.

At noon on the fourth day, Lala Othman stood next to
the old jetty of the port of the gentiles listening to the
rocking of the waves in the recess hollowed out from rock
in which ships had formerly anchored. He spotted two
youths sitting on the sand talking about winds which were
favorable for sailing; the desert wind which parts the sea and
can bring a sailing ship to Athens and the south wind which
can bring it back from there. As the youths rose, so did Lala
Othman who followed them to town.

They passed along the empty port between remnants of
ships, old ropes and broken barrels, walking before a facade
of warehouses which from the outside seemed full and
whose doors were broken down and whose doorways were
strewn with piles of trash.

The youths entered an alleyway and stopped next to a
house. They climbed up a pile of laundry and stuck their
heads through a window. Lala Othman walked around the
house and entered. In a corner of the hall he saw a short old
man, in tattered rags, his hair unkempt, a rope tied about
his chest. The end of the rope was held by a soldier in a
faded uniform. People crowded around. A fat bald man, his
arms covered with tattoos, was throwing dice and covering
them up with his palm. The short old man would guess at
the numbers, saying in a quiet voice: three, six. Or he would
use words which in Sa'ida indicated certain numbers: camel,
twins. All the guesses were right and often with each

guess were heard cries of wonder and sighs among the crowd.

For a minute Lala Othman weighed the validity of the guesses but without seeing the old man close up he knew from the proud smile on the guard's face — like the grin of one watching the antics of a trained ape or dog — that the old man was not cheating. That moment the old man stopped his guessing and stared at him.

"That's the man," said Lala Othman to himself for no reason. He looked in disgust at the crowd filling the hall. The features of the fat man were heavy and imbecilic. The lone sign of any pleasantness about him — his childishness — concealed a dangerous irresponsibility and cruelty. The face of the man serving platters of rice was almost blue, his watery eyes waiting for the moment of forgetfulness. The features of another man told that he was ruled by foul desires. A servant talking to himself was sweeping the room.

"They are more contemptible than the dust," said Lala Othman to himself.

"And now what?" asked the fat man.

"Four, six," answered the old man. Those about had not lost interest in what was happening despite his obvious success.

After a number of moments the old man placed his hand on his brow. The guard said something about fatigue, informed the onlookers that the performance had ended and requested a few coins for the upkeep of the prison. Then he pulled on the rope and the two left.

Lala Othman turned to his neighbor, who told him that the old man was a crazy prisoner who could not remember his name and that the jailer brought him out every once in a while to amuse the passers-by in the caravanserai and the market with his pranks.

Lala Othman was certain that this was the man he sought. He went to the prison, a round building like a tower, its walls thick and its whitewash corroded with salt — a building twisted and distorted from every angle. Lala Othman knocked on the door. A small portal opened above and the guard's head appeared.

"This could be the most important moment of my life," said Lala Othman to himself. He looked at those praying and resting on the mats in the yard of the great mosque, who could be seen from the steps of the prison. Then he followed the guard.

They entered a dark cell. The guard lit two candles and left. Lala Othman looked at the man sitting on a pile of straw.

"Did you come to help me?" asked the old man.

"Who are you?"

The man kept quiet, his head shaking all the time, and he searched the features of the guest.

"I am de la Reina's disciple," he said.

"You are Yehuda Meir?"

"Yes," said the old man his eyes narrow and a smell of sour madness permeated the dark cell. "Yes, I am the last who remained of his disciples and guardians of his secrets and here I am locked in a prison on my sick bed without any medication for the agonies of my body."

As he said this the prisoner sank into silence. Only his head trembled. After a few moments he lifted his head and asked: "Did you come to help me?"

"What do you want?" asked Lala Othman.

"I want to leave here," said Yehuda Meir; "I want to find my teacher."

"Did your teacher not die many years ago?"

The old man drew near and whispered into his ear: "That is all lies. Can you free me from here?"

"Yes. I can," said Lala Othman.

"If so let us leave now, at once, so that my teacher will not grow distant," said Yehuda Meir in a parched voice. Looking at the barred window he put his hand on his heart and collapsed.

Lala Othman put his ear next to the filthy rags but did not hear the slightest flutter. As he was young, he stood for a moment with tear-filled eyes over the opportunity snatched from under his nose. He jumped up, disgustedly kicked the body and raised his head. Between the highest square of bars was seen a lone star.

Lala Othman looked at it apathetically. His bodyguards who had searched for him everywhere stood waiting for him on the prison steps.

"I distributed charity to the poor and needy," Lala Othman told them, thinking about the important posts awaiting him in the future and on the changing fashions in the court of Suleiman, the Magnificient "as one must do before a long journey." He added: "so they say."

The bodyguards and officials laughed and cried out: "Long live Lala Othman!"

In an hour Lala Othman was already aboard, jotting down notes regarding repairs to Port Sa'ida and going over invoices for the supply of fodder and meat to the battalion waiting for him in a Tunis fortress.

Translated by Curtis Arnson

Ring Around the Little Cranes

HAYIM BE'ER

Like most human activity, this story too has its start in a dream.

Quite a few months after I'd finished a lengthy period of reserve duty along the western shore of the Great Bitter Lake, I would still see Fenra often in my dreams.

In those last days of the war I was part of a group whose job was to search out the remains of soldiers who fell in the battle for the Egyptian naval base. Every morning, at dawn, we'd leave our quarters which were next to the Faid morgue and head south on the highway which led to the Nasser factories, overlooking the suburbs of Suez and Abadieh harbor.

We were three in the cab. Mintz sat there wrapped up in himself, twirling his graying beard, his lips moving soundlessly. He'd make sure, he told me one morning, to recite Nachmanides' letter at least once a week. He thumbed through his prayer book and said that reading the letter which Nachmanides sent to his son who lived in Catalonia, seven hundred years ago, would be likely to instill a genuine fear of God in my heart — and the sooner the better.

The captured Egyptian car bumped along ceaselessly over the badly pitted road and I made an effort to read the tiny blurred letters. But when I got to the part where Nachmanides says that you must "always keep thy mind on from whence thou hast come and where thou goest, and that thou art but a worm and a maggot in thy life and even more so in thy death," I closed the book and said that I was perfectly familiar with the passage and I would be better off sparing my eyes.

Mintz went on mumbling and the driver, who had not become involved in our conversation, tried to pick up the army station on the radio, but the voice of the Radio Cairo announcer, with its broken Hebrew, sounded clearly and drowned out the distant voices of the Israeli station. "What a country!" said the driver and left the radio alone. And after a pause he added that that crap was located nearby, just over the hills, and he pointed towards the Genifah Ridge which rose on our right.

We soon turned left, to Fenra, at the spot where the military police had put up an oil drum with the name of the place and a red arrow hurriedly scrawled on it. Mintz woke up, spread out the map and decided where we'd do our searching this time. That was how we carefully surveyed, day after day, the heavily mined area.

Mintz was quick at his work and it was enough for him to spot a jacket collar peeking through the bushes, a button or a seething ant-hill for him to be able to find that "bundle" which was gradually merging with the ground underneath it. The whole length of the road was fenced by barbed-wire and marked by red triangular signs. During the afternoons, after we'd traced the locations of the casualties, some engineering corps people would turn up and blaze a trail for us through the heart of the mined area.

Months after I came back from there, after I'd washed my hands every day with carbolic soap, I'd still be afraid to cuddle my children and I'd still see Fenra in my dreams. Mintz and I were always making our way along an abandoned asphalt road which had weeds sticking up through the cracks, carefully heading for the boat jetty on the lake shore.

While Mintz busied himself with his work I used the field-binoculars to scan the lake, whose shores were also strewn with mines. On that spot, one of the border guards told me, three reservists were killed when they went down to swim and wash their clothes.

I surveyed the lake with the binoculars, starting with five ships which were crowded together like frightened sheep in the middle of the lake. They were anchored motionlessly and only the white-and-red buoys bobbed lightly with the waves. There was no sign of life on board. Then, very slowly, I turned to scan the areas between the ruined buildings on my left.

Everything was close enough to touch — an army mosque made of tin slats and painted in Egyptian camouflage colors, a weathered British shack, a house whose four walls had collapsed completely, leaving an Oriental floor, a table and chair, and a branch of bougainvillaea in the center space, a vigorous bougainvillaea, blossoming, painfully purplish-red, penetrating the house through the window which had buckled along with the wall into which it had been built. And a few steps away, there was a lone wall, the remains of some other house, a wall decorated with brown, burnt sienna and blue drawings of a stern Arab and a fire-breathing dragon, very reminiscent of Paldi's paintings. And then suddenly, from behind the wall, a well-shaven figure wearing a white colonial suit stood up and waved at us with his gloves.

"What're you doing here, Rabbi David," I called out in the dream, and I started walking towards him.

Mintz, who was, as I said, absorbed in the map and the hillocks between the ruins, looked up and yelled: "You want to go back home in a formica coffin? You crazy kid!"

I'd never seen Rabbi David Ledder. He died before I ever appeared on the scene. But for an instant I saw his picture twenty years before, back in the days when his son Mordechai Ledder had advised me to join the ranks of his Nutrition Army.

On that distant Jerusalem afternoon, on my way back from school, making my way home between the houses of Nachlat-Sheva, I saw Mr. Ledder coming out of the Russian bookstore which was in the Sanssoor building. He lifted his eyes to Malinkov's picture in the center of the show-window, surrounded by books in red bindings and adorned with carnations and asparagus stalks. "Those communists," he said to me with a nod when he caught sight of me, "they won't last, but you will," and then he asked if I'd ever heard of Popper-Linkeus.

"The brother of Dr. Pruper of 'Hadassah'?" I asked.

Ledder quietly laughed: "Not Pruper, Popper," and he opened one of the books he was carrying under his arm and showed me a picture of him. "A great man," said Ledder. "Twenty years before Dupres he already knew how to pass an electric current through a metal wire."

He paused for a moment. He gazed at the face with its high forehead — which somehow reminded one of Einstein — and at his stylized signature, and then suggested that we go to the Café Vienna. That was the first time in my life I sat in a café.

He was in high spirits. He told me that that Soviet Zhdanov's face had become very serious and closed when he heard that Ledder wanted to buy Popper-Lynkeus's books. The salesman rejected the books that Ledder showed him and said that it wasn't smart, especially during times like these, to read books that were outdated. And naturally, added the salesman, those books hadn't been translated into Russian and there was no reason to believe that they ever would be.

Ledder pushed his hat back on his head and said that with God's help we would yet live to see the day when, in my parents' grocery store and Mr. Rachlevsky's shop, they would be wrapping olives and cheese in the writings of Stalin and Lenin. This, to my astonishment, did in fact come about a few years later, as I'll tell you further on.

The waitress appeared and Ledder ordered two bottles of "Aqua Destila" and some coconut flakes and added that she should make sure that the glasses were properly washed. He didn't want to drink from a glass on which some tart had left traces of her lipstick. The waitress's mouth gaped open in surprise and Ledder asked her unblinkingly if she was as Viennese as the name of the café in which she worked.

She said "yes" and Ledder went on to ask if she'd ever eaten in the vegetarian restaurant in Vienna across from the university.

"When was that?" asked the waitress.

"Back in '19."

"My good sir," she said, offended, "in '19 I was still in school."

"But children sit in cafés too," said Ledder, pushing the napkin-holder over to me.

"This is Palestine," declared the waitress and started to light a cigarette.

Ledder levelled his gaze at her and remarked astringently that in Vienna, on the other hand, the restaurants were very high class and even the clients were not allowed to smoke.

"Maybe coffee and some fresh strudel?" she asked coldly, smoothing down her starched apron.

Ledder thought things over and said that it was a great pity that Mr. Prevrov had closed down his vegetarian restaurant near the Egged bus station, and since he had no choice he ordered two cups of hot water and some natural honey.

The waitress went off and Ledder related that for a year, while he was in Vienna, he'd been accustomed to getting together in that restaurant with the "Coconut Covenant Association."

"The Coconut Covenant," he repeated when he saw the astounded look on my face, and he told me that the members of the association regarded the coconut as man's natural food and that they had planned to set out for one of the islands in the Pacific, to leave the customs of civilization behind and make their home in the heart of Nature.

"And they would've climbed trees naked, like monkeys," I couldn't restrain myself from saying.

"And what's wrong with monkeys," Ledder said, ending the argument and remarking that we ought to be realistic and not cling to the past or indulge in unimportant theological debates. He took out his Parker pen and began writing slowly and meticulously on the café's engraved paper napkins: "Popper-Lynkeus's Social Minimum Program." When he finished he looked up and asked me if in my opinion economic liberalism had solved the problem of the starving millions.

Since in those days I hadn't yet heard of David Ricardo and John Stuart Mill, just as I didn't know who Popper-Lynkeus was, I simply continued to stare as if bewitched by the strange emblem which was pinned to his lapel, an emblem whose significance I was not yet acquainted with. It was a white Shield of David with a five-pointed star embedded in its center. Ledder, who apparently interpreted my silence as agreement born of weakness, went ahead and asked if to my mind the Beveridge Report had at all decreased the number of elderly men and women who died of hunger and loneliness throughout the United Kingdom, those same old people who were left alone in their rooms day after day with only a dog to watch over them and to whine faithfully and persistently at the sight of their dead faces.

Many years later I was the youngest of a small group of people who clustered about in the Avichail Hospital yard, behind the courthouse, waiting for Ledder's funeral. I stood next to the well-kept garden of the Russian nuns, working my shoes into the layer of gravel that covered the narrow area, when I became aware of Riklin's presence. The old grave-digger put his arm around my shoulder and with his other hand traced a wide semi-circle in the air. "They all die, *mein kind,*" said Riklin as his eyes slowly passed over the mourners until they came to rest on the very curly-headed seamstress who stood near us, crushing a sprig of rosemary between her fingers. "They all die," repeated Riklin in such a loud voice that I was afraid someone might hear him.

He covertly took a bite from a bar of dietetic chocolate. "But each day they come to us only in small servings. He knows we couldn't possibly bury them all in one day," he finished, rolling his eyes heavenwards.

I asked Riklin how Ledder had died. He turned serious and said that someone who'd been Bar Mitzvah for only two years shouldn't ask such questions, and anyway, he added, there was no need for me to be going to funerals.

The curly-headed seamstress slowly moved towards us. "Mrs. Schechter, would you like a piece of chocolate?" offered Riklin to Behirah the seamstress. She shook her head and said that it was shameful to eat at a funeral. Riklin burst out laughing and said that if he were to listen to her, he would have died long ago of starvation.

In the doorway of the purification room a figure with rolled-up sleeves appeared. Riklin slapped me on the shoulder and disappeared through the narrow door. A few minutes later Ledder was taken out, covered with a prayer shawl. His belly protruded like a little mound and for a moment it seemed as if it couldn't be Ledder at all, since he had always been skinny.

The yellowing prayer shawl emphasized the outlines of the corpse beneath it. I had an urge to look at its face but I turned my eyes away. Twenty years later, at a time when I was steeped day and night in those sweetly-sick odors, surrounded by faces reeking with blood and vomit, I would still feel nauseated at the memory of the hinted-at form of that corpse in the sunny Russian Compound in Jerusalem.

A stir moved through the congregation and a dignified Jew dressed in what was a combination of old Yishuv and Mid-European doctor-rabbiner styles, separated himself from the group with small steps. This was Rabbi Ziffer, about whose piety my aunt Zivia had more than once cast some doubt. "That rotter," my aunt used to say, "he drank five-o'clock-tea in London with the English ladies and here he drags angels down from heaven." She'd known him in his youth and she used to say that his smoking habit was so severe that every Friday he would fill bottles with tobacco smoke to inhale on the Sabbath.

Rabbi Ziffer cleared his throat and began in a low tone: " 'And Mordechai went out from the presence of the King,' that eminent man, now deceased, laid out before us, Rabbi Mordechai Ledder, blessed be his memory, who went out from the presence of the King and from the presence of the Maker of the World. In the Talmud we find that . . ."

But I'm putting the cart before the horse.

During the course of that far off afternoon Ledder had already managed to dispense with economic liberalism and was now on his way to venting his anger on Marxism. When the waitress came over he cut off the flow of his speech. On the table in front of us she put two glasses of water and two saucers of honey and she was able to get away before Ledder tasted the water and grimaced.

As he stirred the honey into the water he added that a society which would like to be informed by justice must first of all concern itself with basic necessities and not with strudels. He took a sip from his drink and remarked that a Nutrition Squad ought to be set up. "This army," said Ledder, "will supply basic foodstuffs to the population, both in cooked and uncooked form. If a person wants to, he can take his ration home and cook it himself; if not, he can eat in the public dining rooms, just as we are today." He added: "The public dining rooms will be under public supervision and those aging Viennese ladies will do exactly as they're told."

The water in the glass in front of me was still clear and Ledder urged me to follow his example. On the green-checkered tablecloth, on the spot where Ledder had laid his pen, a blue ink-stain was spreading outwards. Ledder noticed this, placed an ash-tray over the stain and stated that one must not allow external matters to distract one from the main issue.

When the youngsters finish their military service, said Ledder, with a smile on his face, every one of them will be entitled to a life of freedom and will have the right to spend his own life as he wishes.

I squirmed restlessly in my chair. I was afraid that my mother would be worried and out looking for me in the streets. I started to get up. Ledder ordered me to sit down and asked if there wasn't, in my opinion, something coercive about his plan. I nodded my head and Ledder seemed to have anticipated this. "And the army, your army, it's not coercive?" he exclaimed. "Here no one ever thinks things through to the end."

He sipped at his mead and said that these ideas had been well-tested. "We're standing here with our two feet on the ground of reality," and the problem was to gather at least twenty realistic people together who would be sufficiently intelligent to want to set up the Popper-Lynkeus state.

At this point Ledder fixed his eyes on me and said that he wouldn't delay me any longer but that the day was not far off when he would be the director of the "Ministry of Survival" which would be the highest body dealing with producing and distributing minimum requirements. And he added that the decision had already been taken to assign me, in spite of my youthfulness, the rank of "First Supplier," should I in fact agree to join his army.

"Think it over," he said and the hint of a smile showed on his bloodless lips. He scrabbled about in his leather briefcase which was full of receipt booklets and collection boxes to be hung on the wall for donations to the school for the blind where he worked as a fund raiser, and he pulled out a little green-bound book that had a green dove carrying an olive sprig in its mouth on its cover.

"Take this, read Dorion's book and Einstein's preface. Yes, Professor Einstein; and find out what kind of man Popper-Lynkeus really was."

But Ledder didn't let me thumb through the book. He opened the briefcase which was on the seat between us, stuffed in " An End to the War of Survival" and said that instead of running off to the corner kiosk at recess to eat pastry and drink soda water, I would do better to sit down in the schoolyard, in the shade of the trees, and read this book.

Ledder got up and before he turned to go he asked me where I went to school.

At home they weren't too fond of Ledder.

Once every two months Ledder used to slip up on us and unhook from the wall the yellow box with the picture of a little girl with unkempt hair and a little boy wearing a beret — both of them blind. He would empty the box onto the table and pile the coins into little towers while talking to my mother. Once he asked her if her sister Elka who had gone to South Africa thirty years previously was still as sweet as sugar. My mother made a face and left the room. Ledder swept the coins into his already packed cloth bag and commented that someone who had never gone out into the great world could have no understanding of life.

In the evening, when we went to Ahuva's, my mother didn't restrain herself and told her friend what Ledder had said. Ahuva said that he was a jerk and that even sheep and goats should beware of him, and that it wasn't for no reason that he was working where he was working, because there he'd crawl through the rooms and feel up the legs and young flesh of those poor little girls who had never seen the glory of the world.

Ma pulled me over to her and gestured to Ahuva not to talk that way in front of the boy.

"The apple doesn't fall far from the tree," said Ahuva, and a blush rose on her cheeks.

During the World War Ledder's father, that same Rabbi
David who had appeared in my dreams, was an agent for the
Turks, and Chaim Segal, Ahuva's first husband, was his sub-
agent. The Turks wanted to stop-up the Suez Canal with
thousands of bags of earth and thereby block the passage of
English warships. Ledder and Chaim Segal went around
among the sick and starving populace and bought up all
their clothes dirt-cheap; and then for good money Ledder
sold the clothing to the Turks who made bags out of the
cloth.

Back in those days, when crowns and ornaments were
taken off Torah scrolls and sold by weight as scrap silver,
old clothes weren't worth much. But forty years later
Ahuva would still say that Ledder's father swindled those
poor beggars, that he simply bewitched them and got them
to strip naked. She would dry an eye and add in a whisper
that he also bewitched Chaim, who should only rest in
peace, as well as the famous businessman Mr. Perlman, and
even those stupid Turks who believed that the rags wouldn't
rot in the waters of the Suez Canal.

That winter — which I spent in the Sinai Desert and along
the shores of Great Bitter Lake, when I crossed the Canal
back and forth near Deir Seuer — I couldn't help but smile
at the sight of the putrid corpses of enemy soldiers which
were dragged up from the bottom of the Canal, with their
canvas uniforms rotted away to the point of being un-
recognizable.

After the war too, Chaim didn't stray far from Ledder,
who had grown close to the extremely orthodox circles in
Jerusalem. Ahuva said that at their get-togethers the rabbis
made fun of the silly old man. But on the broadsides which
were pinned up all over Jerusalem, his name was prefaced
with the title "Spokesman and Advocate," and he, knowing

fluent English, wrote memoranda to the British governor, negotiated with the cabinet in London and corresponded with members of parliament and newspaper editors. In particular Ledder was of use to them whenever they met with the governor. In the single photograph remaining from that period, and which I spotted on the sideboard when I made a quick visit to Rabbi Ledder's son's room, I saw Dr. De Haan, who was murdered a few months after the picture was taken, Chaim Segal and Ledder leaving the governor's residence. In the center stood a tight-mouthed De Haan, a large skull-cap on his head and a bristly beard surrounding his face. Especially eye-catching was his tie, which had been knotted too tightly. On his right stood Rabbi Ledder, smooth-shaven, wearing a white suit and waving his gloves at an Arab policeman. Off to the side, a bit awkwardly, stood Chaim Segal, a tattered briefcase in his hand and Ledder's jacket over his arm.

Rabbi David, Ledder's father, occasionally traveled to London, to Vienna, and to the large Agudat-Yisrael convention at Marienbad, where he would sharpen his brains on matters of Jewish law with the heads of yeshivot and great biblical scholars; and at night, added Ahuva in a whisper, he would go to cabarets. This was while the farthest her Chaim ever got from Jerusalem was to Lower Motza where he went to draw water for baking Passover matzah.

During the forties Segal was beaten to death by some toughs while picketing against voting for the National Committee on election day, warning the public not to participate in the elections. Three years after he died Ahuva married Benjamin Haris, who was now standing in the kitchen, cooking garlic in milk — a potion, so my father used to say, for virility.

My mother and Ahuva spoke in whispers. And Benjamin, who sensed that his wife's Great Love had returned to haunt his nest, appeared in the kitchen doorway.

"Churchill's a Jew," he declared and tapped the spoon rimmed with milk curds on the nearest mezuzah.

My mother said that everyone knows that Churchill is an English goy, born and bred, but Benjamin persisted and said that only a Jew would name his daughter Sarah.

Ahuva sighed and upbraided her husband, telling him to get back in the kitchen and watch that the milk doesn't boil over and dirty up the stove.

When Benjamin vanished back into the kitchen my mother said that if she'd had a writer's talents, she would have written a book about Ledder. Ahuva smirked and said that the Ledder family's life wasn't all that important and it could hardly be made into a serial for the "Amerikaner" magazine but, she added, asking my mother, who was a few years older than she was, "Why did the zadik's son go off to Vienna after the British came to Palestine?"

My mother was astonished that her friend's memory had faded to such an extent and she said that the whole city knew that young Ledder had been captivated by two Chinese women.

"The Chinks stood in the Alliance school-yard," said my mother, "and removed white worms from the eyes of the little Mission girls. No, not with tweezers, just with glass rods. And Ledder stood there from early morning, smoking English cigarettes and speaking German, and after a week he went off to Beirut."

This episode from his distant past was hinted at by Ledder himself one day, on our way back from the central post office at the end of Jaffa Street. He claimed that he was forced to trudge all the way down there because the

tellers in the Mea Shearim Quarter post office were not
sufficiently cultured to know either the Latin alphabet or a
little geography. A letter sent to Lambarène, said Ledder,
would get to Africa via Rio de Janeiro. But the central post
office tellers, who had received a British education, would
give a letter addressed to Dr. Albert Schweitzer the respect
it deserved.

Ledder told me that in his three-page letter he was
appealing to the aged doctor to take on the eminent
position of serving as the governor of the Lynkeussian state.

There was no doubt, said Ledder, that someone who
directly served humanity with such deep and continual
sympathy for the living would certainly reply to his letter in
the positive.

Ledder lavishly praised the renowned physician, but
when we passed the "Zion" Bible Shop on the corner of the
Street of the Prophets and Munbez Street, he suddenly
remarked that the Mizrachi Organization and the "Agudah"
would undoubtedly object to the appointment of a
Christian doctor and would suggest a Jewish scholar in his
stead.

"The Missionaries are good people," he said and told of
how in his younger days he had known two nuns who had
come from China and saved a lot of sick people, until they
themselves were stricken with a serious eye disease, went
blind and ended their days in a little nunnery in Italy.

He became lost in thought and only when we reached
Strauss Street, near Bikur-Cholim Hospital, Ledder said that
time would tell and that there was nothing to fear from the
religious Jews, and he asked me if I would accompany him
to Peres Street where he was to meet the seamstress who
was preparing uniforms for his Nutrition Brigade.

Behirah the Seamstress's good-heartedness was very well-

known. "It's lucky for her," my father used to say a few
times a year, "that she's so ugly." And a few times a year
my mother would hastily have to shut him up. After she
would leave our house, late in the evening, after a long, hard
day of sewing, my father would look at the skirt she'd made
from an old American-style suit, at my trousers which she'd
sewn from one of my mother's skirts, and at the sheets
made from French sugar sacks, and say that in Russia they
would have sent her to Siberia for such sloppy work.

I toyed with the wooden thread spools and colored in the
eyes of the whales which were stamped on them. In the
kitchen the kettle was boiling and my father whispered to
my mother while she was pouring out the tea that in his
opinion, Behirah must enjoy being stimulated by the
rubbing of her legs together while operating the sewing
machine, because otherwise he couldn't understand how she
could stand sewing all day long. My mother got angry and
told him to stop bothering her and to get up already and
close the shutters.

Now Ledder was knocking on the door which had a green
enamel sign tacked on it. In the middle of the sign there was
a red "S" and in the center of the "S" there was a picture of
a woman bent over a Singer sewing machine. A skilled hand,
apparently that of the Jerusalem artist Isaac Beck, had
added in white "Scroll" type, "Behirah Schechter — Quality
Seamstress."

Mrs. Schechter opened the door a crack and when she
saw Ledder she said she was busy measuring a lady client
and if the matter was urgent then he should wait in the
kitchen.

"*Ingele, teirer ingele,*" she exclaimed when she saw me.
"Your mother's here."

From the big room at the end of the hall I saw my

mother peering out in alarm, wearing only a bra-and-corset.

"What's happened to your father," she asked, almost yelling.

"No, he's come with Ledder," said Behirah.

"So then finish the outfit the way it is," my mother shot back, and a minute later emerged from the depths of the room, hurriedly dressed.

All the way home she didn't say a word and she didn't look at me. She grasped my hand firmly and hummed without pause:

"Ring around the little cranes,
Buzz, buzz, buzz, the busy bees;
Circle, circle, little cranes."

At home my father was waiting for us, and as for cranes, those I saw for the first time twenty years later, on the banks of the Bitter Lake, walking about among the palm trees, just where I dreamed, months afterward, that I saw Ledder's father waving at me with his white gloves.

Translated by Nancy Elkin

Night

ESTHER RAAB

To be still
stillness of stone
stopped of breath
the rock's secret silence
in your mountains, knowing
to hear
your heart's blood dripping
in darkness
like a faucet with a broken valve
to listen
to the throb of an abscess
in wounds of the time
swollen and screaming
to feel
your country's convulsion, it groans
with strings pulled
between earth and heaven
flapping of dove's wings
struggling afraid
suddenly
nightmare
in leaves of the oak
cling to old scars
and new ones
and wait for a ray of light
from above
for a cry of a blackbird
fast asleep
in the morning.

Translated by Shirley Kaufman
with Shlomit Rimmon

Place of Fire

ZELDA

Mountain air, living air,
breathing lover—
beg mercy for us
from the Most-High.
Place of fire,
place of weeping,
place of madness—
even bride and groom
beg the mercy of the heavens
lest the horizon crumble.
Dogs and cats are alarmed.
Only in the plants
the nectars don't darken
a step away from the abyss.
Only in the flowers
the sweetness won't retreat
a step away from death.
For the plants are a different nation
from us,
except for the olive trees
which are sad and wise
like people.
And when a foreign, enemy king
crushes our ties to the city
upon whose neck
a loving prophet hung
sapphires, turquoise, and rubies—
the silver treetops tremble

like my heart.
And when a foreign, enemy king
crushes our awesome love
for the city of David—
the roots of the olive tree
hear a small soldier's blood
whispering from the dust:
The city is crouching on my life.

                              Translated by Marcia Falk

Jerusalem, the Place in Which All Remember

YEHUDA AMICHAI

Jerusalem, the place in which all remember
they forgot something
but they can't remember what they forgot.

This is my city where the instruments of my dreams fill
like divers' oxygen tanks to dive.

The holiness in her
changes at times to love.

And the questions asked in these hills
are as always: Did you see my sheep?
Did you see my shepherd?

And the door of my house is open
like a grave from which people rose to life.

Translated by Harold Schimmel

Our Baby Was Weaned in the First Days

YEHUDA AMICHAI

Our baby was weaned in the first days
of the war. And I ran to look out
on the terrible desert.

At night I returned again to see him
sleep. He begins to forget his mother's nipples
and will go on forgetting until the next war.

Thus, still small, his hopes are stopped
and his claims opened, that won't close again.

Translated by Harold Schimmel

Anatomy of a War

T. CARMI

This is the author's apology:

I said to my face —
Stay with me.
But it widened suddenly
like a lake
struck by rocks from the sky,
and it didn't return to me.

I said to my dreams —
The night is yours to rule.
But in droves they invaded my day.
The sun rose, the sun set,
and I couldn't tell.

I said to my name —
Stick with me.
I kept a signed photograph in my pocket,
fingered it endlessly.
Too much, it seems.

I was stripped of face, day, and name.

That was the author laying himself bare;
that was his apology.

Translated by Marian Falk

Serpent, Serpent

T. CARMI

Serpent, serpent,
go tell the Supreme Serpent
we're all choking underneath our old skins.

Serpent, serpent,
go tell the Supreme Serpent
our baby eyes are hardening in our foreheads,

our old hands are like rusty pliers,
our old mouths are like a shoe in the desert,
our old tongues like deformed keys,
the old venom seethes in our lungs.

Serpent, serpent,
go tell the Supreme Serpent
to give us back the seasons of the year,
summer and spring, winter and fall

and the moon at night.

Translated by Marcia Falk

Observations at the End of a Journey

ABBA KOVNER

I wanted to be born at the farthest limit of the world.
I'll explore it, I said to myself,
biting big chunks from it.
And when I want, I'll go
straight to the core.
This is the way of the world I thought in my innocence,
round and around the layers of peel
until the taste becomes certain.

And you were within me. Seven times more clear
than the light of my eyes. Do you find me an absolute fool
if, at the opening of an unknown field,
with a butterfly net in my hand,
I still kneel
in front of grasshoppers and bugs.

Translated by Shirley Kaufman

Behold how the nations

AMIR GILBOA

Behold how the nations gather together
and come to thee stand on your threshold
intrigue in their hands a time of exact calculation
marked minute by minute until the hour
runs out their spirits run out to see
your spirits flying. Signs
will be drawn in the air they'll imagine they see them
rising a remnant from a page of their sins. Their covenant
of blood will ask for your blood to be rain
a blessing quenching the thirst of their souls. Curse them.

That such are their lives. That their lives are hostile
to the spirit of your life. Guard your soul guard it
against the cursed hour.

Translated by Shirley Kaufman
with Shlomit Rimmon

If you get up and leave

AMIR GILBOA

If you get up and leave your country
and your homeland you will not leave even if you go far
the migration of birds will bring painful greetings
from a burning summer in a winter wasted and eaten by
    whiteness
and your longing will stretch over distance jointed
by a steel thread strong and unseen
that butchers the flesh and pours in the soul sweet poisons
of vintage wine spilled with sorrow
on a land of poison hemlock. And it will be like wormwood
in your mouth only a last memory left to recover
an old taste bestowed on you but withheld
from your sons and whether they greet you
in the ancient language or in the new
both will be sickening to your ears
because you will hear it in a strange foreign country.

Translated by Shirley Kaufman
with Shlomit Rimmon

Love Song

ANTON SHAMMAS

In the beginning, air penetrates
Under the locked door. I put my feet up on the hassock
As though waiting for the flood. I write
About hardbound love. What's

God doing now? Noting in braille
That I'm blinking, that the room
Is a wet bird. The weatherman
Expects rain. I don't. I vainly

Expect your voice from afar.
Dreams sit on the edge of my bed
As if they were in a waiting-room. Air penetrates
Under the locked door. They lift their legs

Expecting sleep. I don't. In this condition
Sleep won't recognize me. The weatherman
Sitting up there in his tower waits for rain
Now maybe he isn't thinking of me. I think

Of the verse, "My beloved will sleep betwixt my breasts."
I think about the zipper which is in your flesh
The length of your body,
Like a sleeping bag.

Translated by Betsy Rosenberg

Sitting on the Rail

ANTON SHAMMAS

Sitting on a Tel Aviv rooftop in the sun
On a cold day. Old pensionaries. A limp
Crane tries to lift the town
And the day fallen down into a cup of coffee.

Two cries for help, you and I,
In this sinking city,
Sit on the rail
Fishing for quiet with love-hooks.

Translated by Betsy Rosenberg

In Camera

MEIR WIESELTIER

Until she came I danced alone
and danced alone until I heard
the sound of her steps.

And when she came
I stopped. All the tracks of my dancing in the room
shrank to one stare.

She had forgotten to wash off her night-mask.

She went through the town like that,
not taking it off.
She climbed the stairs like that, she rang the bell like that,
    she entered like that:
she bought, it seems
lots of expensive make-up
and now it's weighing her down.
And she can arrange it in a circle and stand in the middle
    and smile.

And the night-mask
grips the smile
and serves it up with a clenched fist.

And music, music
endlessly played in the background
can't stop.

And I, who stopped, stretch myself.
Soon the ceiling.
And my head will bump, will break through, will see

the whole town
except for her.

Translated by Shirley Kaufman
with Shlomit Rimmon

Fruit

MEIR WIESELTIER

A burning cigarette tossed into the tree
at five in the morning
blooms for a minute in a red brilliance between the leaves.

You might as well say it's the fruit of the tree
(tobacco, paper), a different tree
granted, but why be pedantic?
The fruit burns, the fruit fizzles out.

And man has his fill for a minute, then he doesn't.

Translated by Shirley Kaufman
with Shlomit Rimmon

Anemones

REUVEN BEN-YOSEF

Just a bit and again we go out to anemones
Pulsating in blue, in purple, and especially
Red, which the Greeks thought was
The blood of Adonis, a handsome lad, slightly resembling
David our shepherd, but on Adonis
Never fell the wrath of a king, old and jealous—
But ᵣather an efficient wild boar. Others say
The blood is of rash Aphrodite
Whose pearly leg was scratched during the hasty
Search for her gored love.
Thus or otherwise, they speared and stabbed the youth
And turned his spilled blood to a flower, the one I love.
The first time I saw a field of anemones
Was on the hills above the Kinneret, towards evening,
During an operation defined as an exercise in mine-laying,
Which was really a bitter battle against rocks, with antiquated
Arms called shovels. The sun
Already ran off, and like a full moon
The Kinneret became filled with the most exquisite
    brightness,
And also from up high it was thrilling to look at
The blue, the purple, and especially the red of
The anemones in the midst of the practice area.
We were careful while digging, not to uproot
Even one marvel, and we laid training mines

And hung signs, "beware, mines" on the wire,
And we grouped from afar, with the Kinneret below us
Like a beloved's navel, from which we drink
To life, whenever not off to war.

Translated by Curtis Arnson

Forever

GAD AVIASAF

Not like a snake on the road that suddenly drops
from a tree to coil around the neck of a fleeing stag
and not with the cunning of foxes
that split the entire night with sharp-edged faces
and not with the wisdom of owls
that choose chaff from wheat when how and where
they should fall on the nest of their prey in the night

but like this: open eyed, eye for an eye
with conditions equally decreed. Flesh and soul
the game should be played from start to end neatly
since the hands of the players will bleed like waters of the sea
in a splendor

which by its nature is forever lost.

Translated by Shirley Kaufman
with Judy Levy

When Children Close Their Eyes

GAD AVIASAF

When children close their eyes
they say the lights are off

tiny swindlers

nothing escapes their watchful intelligence
for when eyesight gets dim we discover suddenly
a new trembling expanse of a holiday eve that till now
moved in the clothing of sound but by nature
secreted itself
in the shadows of trees.

And this is the secret: what sings best will shatter first.

So with the faces darkened the players leave the stage
and one by one they hide behind the curtain.

Cheers of silence

the voice of the turtle has turned to glass.

Translated by Shirley Kaufman

Balloons

DAN PAGIS

Balloons at a party hug each other
between snakes of paper,
and humbly accept
their limit, the ceiling of the room.
They are prepared for every hint,
careful to obey the slightest breeze.
But even these meek of the earth
their time is coming.
Suddenly their souls fly off
with a startled squeal
or they burst
in a single explosion.
Then the rubber corpses lie torn
on the edge of a filthy carpet,
and the souls wander
between worlds, almost as high as your nose.

Translated by Shirley Kaufman
with Shlomit Rimmon

Jason's Grave in Rehavia

DAN PAGIS

Jason, wily seaman,
Secret counsellor to King Jannia
Pretends he was buried
Far from the sea,
In a handsome grave
In a Holy City
Room within room, he is buried, adorned by arches and pillars
Glory and peace eternal were carved for him in the lime-stone.

The grave is empty.
Only the form of a ship
Turned stone on the wall.
Overhead kingdoms fell
New men went down to Hades.

But Jason slips away again and again
Out of the empty wall
(Cuts through the sea of air
Maintaining absolute radio silence)

And smuggles, as always, with great profit
Very expensive contraband:
Sun of water
Silk of wind
Marble of foam.

Translated by Ezra Spicehandler

You Have No Right

ITAMAR YAOZ-KEST

Here
Even to hate the equipment of death
You have no right—

The eternal khaki
Of your uniform
That suddenly puts on your shape
At dark,
And while you still believe you're just dreaming
It leaves the house
Without a call-up
In open green cars
Making for the fire-flickering line.

The green line, the purple line, the black line — you're
    surrounded
As by the rivers of your childhood deep with death,
And a hand of the past now fearfully tunes the radio
To the end of this imaginary summer,
Until
On a rickety chair by the doorway
Sits
Peace
Like a woman hanging her head,
Listening to the evil premonitions in her heart
With the black troops of war news dancing on air—

Here
Even to hate the equipment of death
You have no right.

Translated by Reuven Ben-Yosef

Death; She Was Always Here

YONA WALLACH

It's not true that death is a lump like this, or a blow.
So much like a cloth veil, lifted,
like this he comes slowly, even like a bride.
The journey is private, it's true, listen
to what happens to me, what happens to you.
I'm not trapped here in any abstraction,
but all right, for me, death is like a bridal veil,
I don't speak later on the chariot,
there's this echo on the journey,
someone's disputing this theory,
I'm not involved when I pose a question
there's someone who keeps moving, and in poetry?

Oh, freedom, (my work, her work)
Oh, wind, where are you going, looking like the wind's soul,

you ask me later about her substance,
excuse me, but you seem to deafen yourself to her,
"How long ago was this?" only it's not a guess,
your journey, your death, the same carriage, it's
my death, the death I build, private, her privacy,
don't drop like fowl to her hand with no reply,
she was always here, an obverse view in my land, in her land.

Translated by Leonore Gordon

NOTES ON AUTHORS

SHMUEL YOSEF AGNON (1888-1970) was the 1966
Nobel Laureate in Literature. *Wartime in Leipzig* is taken
from the posthumously-published novel, *In Mr. Lublin's
Store* (Tel Aviv, 1975). Written in the 1960s, it is a
sample of Agnon's skill at its peak.

YEHUDA AMIHAI (1924–   ) was born in Germany and
came to Eretz Israel in 1936. He is well known as a poet,
novelist, and playwright who has been widely translated
into English, German and French. The poems here are
from the cycle, *Jerusalem*. The latest volume of translations of Amihai's poetry is *Songs of Jerusalem and
Myself*, Harper & Row, 1974.

AHARON APPELFELD was born in Czernovitz in 1932
and came to Eretz Israel in 1947. He has published a
number of collections of short stories and two novels. His
main theme is the Holocaust. *Badenheim 1939* originally
appeared in *Ariel* 35, 1974.

GAD AVIASAF is a Tel Aviv poet who has published one
volume of poetry, and has a second in preparation. The
translation of "Forever" first appeared in *Ariel* 41, 1976.

HAYIM BE'ER was born in Jerusalem in 1945. He has
published poems and literary reviews and has recently
turned to prose fiction. The story here first appeared in
the newspaper, *Ma'ariv*.

YITZHAK BEN-NER was born in 1937. Ben-Ner's first
novel, *The Man From There* has been translated into

English (Tel Aviv, Sabra Books), French, Spanish, and Japanese. *A Village Death* is the title-story of his new collection of short stories (Tel Aviv, Am Oved, 1976).

REUVEN BEN-YOSEF was born in New York in 1937. He came to Eretz Israel in 1959. He has published several volumes of verse and a novel. The poem here first appeared in *Modern Hebrew Literature*.

T. CARMI was born in New York in 1925 and came to Eretz Israel in 1947. He has published several collections of poetry. The poems here are numbers 5 and 6 from the cycle, *The Author's Apology* from the book of that name (Tel Aviv, 1974). Carmi has been extensively translated into English. Most recently translations of his poems appeared in the series *"Penguin Modern European Poets,"* 1976.

AMIR GILBOA was born in the USSR in 1917 and came to Eretz Israel in 1937. He began to publish poetry in 1941. The poems here translated are from the series *Recognition Burning* which appeared in the literary periodical *Moznayim*.

ABBA KOVNER was born in 1918 and came to Eretz Israel in 1945, when he joined Kibbutz Ein Ha-Horesh, his present home. Kovner has been widely translated into English and other languages. The poem here appeared as part of the series of "Observations" and is dated July 23, 1975. Selected poems of Kovner have been published in English translation in the Penguin series (1971).

DAN PAGIS was born in Bukovina in 1930 and came to Eretz Israel in 1946. Pagis is professor of Medieval Hebrew Literature at the Hebrew University. The poems are from his collection *Brain* (Tel Aviv, 1976). Translations of Pagis' poetry have recently been published in the Penguin series (1976).

ESTHER RAAB was born in Petach Tikvah in 1899. She has published poetry for over 50 years. "Night" appeared in the literary supplement of the newspaper *Davar*.

ANTON SHAMMAS was born in the Upper Galilee village of Fassuta in 1950. He has written poetry in both Hebrew and Arabic. The translations here are reprinted from *Ariel*. They appeared in his Hebrew collection *Hard Cover* (Tel Aviv, 1974).

DAN TSALKA was born in Warsaw in 1936 and came to Israel in 1957. Tsalka has published poetry, a novel, and short stories. He has edited a poetry series, a newspaper literary supplement, and an arts quarterly. The story here first appeared in the literary journal *Siman Kriyah*, 3.

YONA WALLACH began publishing poetry in 1963. The poem here is from her latest volume, *Collected Poems* (Tel Aviv, 1976).

MEIR WIESELTIER was born in Moscow in 1941 and came to Israel in 1949. Both the poems translated here are from his fifth volume of verse *Something Optimistic, the Making of Poems*, (Tel Aviv, 1976).

ITAMAR YAOZ-KEST was born in Hungary in 1934 and came to Israel in 1951. He has published a number of volumes of poetry and prose and is editor of the *EKED* publishing company. The poem here is from *13 Poems from the Hinterland* (Tel Aviv, 1974).

ZELDA (Shneurson) was born in Russia and came to Israel as a child with her family. Her first book of poems was published in 1967, followed by collections in 1971 and 1975. The poem here is from the volume *Do Not Distance* (Tel Aviv, 1975).

ACKNOWLEDGMENTS

The publishers are grateful to the authors represented in this volume for permission to include their works; to Schocken Publishing House Ltd., Tel Aviv, for permission to include *Wartime in Leipzig,* from S.Y. Agnon's posthumously-published book, *In Mr. Lublin's Store;* and to Siman Kriah Publishers for permission to include "Death; She Was Always Here," by Yona Wallach.

Our thanks are also due to the following translators and publications for permission to use their copyrighted works: Marcia Falk for "Place of Fire," by Zelda and "This is the Author's Apology" and "Serpent, Serpent," by T. Carmi, from the series, "The Author's Apology"; Shirley Kaufman for "Forever," by Gad Aviasaf, first published in *Ariel* 41; Betsy Rosenberg for *Badenheim 1939,* by Aharon Appelfeld, first published in *Ariel* 35 and "Love Song" and "Sitting on the Rail," by Anton Shammas, first published in *Ariel* 33-4; Harold Schimmel for "Jerusalem, the Place in Which All Remember," and "Our Baby Was Weaned in the First Days," by Yehuda Amichai; *Ariel* for *Badenheim 1939,* and the poems by Gad Aviasaf and Anton Shammas; *Modern Hebrew Literature,* Vol. I, no. 2, which first published the poem "Anemones," by Reuven Ben Yosef, translated by Curtis Arnson.